Tennessee

*To Flynn,
Go Vols,
Go God!
Ed McMinn*

Daily Devotions for Die-Hard Kids

Volunteers

TO PARENTS/GUARDIANS FROM THE AUTHOR

DAILY DEVOTIONS FOR DIE-HARD KIDS is an adaptation of our DAILY DEVOTIONS FOR DIE-HARD FANS series. It is suggested for children ages 6 to 12, but that guideline is, of course, flexible. Only the parents or other adults can appraise the spiritual maturity of their children.

The devotions are written with the idea that a parent or adult will join the children to act as a mentor and spiritual guide for each devotion and the discussion that may ensue. The devotions seek to engage the child by capitalizing on his or her interest in the particular collegiate team the family follows. The interest in college sports is thus an oblique and somewhat tricky way, if you will, to lead your children to reading the Bible and learning about God, Jesus, and faith.

Each devotion contains a short Bible reading (except for occasional longer stories that must be read in their entirety), a paraphrase of the most pertinent scripture verse, a true Volunteer sports story, and a theological discussion that ties everything together through a common theme. The devotion then concludes with a suggested activity that is based on the theme of the day. I tie each day's theological message to a child's life by referring to such aspects as school, household chores, video games, and relations with parents, siblings, and teachers, etc.

The devotions are intended to be fun for both the adult and the child, but they are also intended to be attempts to spark interest in quite serious matters of faith and living a godly life. A point of emphasis throughout the book is to impress upon the child that faith is not just for the times when the family gathers for formal worship in a particular structure, but rather is for every moment of every day wherever he or she may be.

Our children are under attack by the secular world as never before. It is a time fraught with danger for the innocence and the faith of our most precious family members. I pray that this book will provide your children with a better understanding of what it means to be a Christian. I also pray that this book will help lay the foundation for what will be a lifelong journey of faith for your children. May God bless you and your family.

ED MCMINN

Volunteers

Daily Devotions for Die-Hard Kids: Tennessee Volunteers
© 2017 Ed McMinn; Extra Point Publishers; P.O. Box 871; Perry GA 31069

To order books or for more information, visit us at www.die-hardfans.com
Cover design by John Powell/Slynn McMinn; Interior design by Slynn McMinn
Every effort has been made to identify copyright holders. Any omissions
are unintentional. Extra Point Publishers should be notified in writing
immediately for full acknowledgement in future editions.

DAILY DEVOTIONS FOR DIE-HARD FANS

ACC
CLEMSON TIGERS
DUKE BLUE DEVILS
FSU SEMINOLES
GA. TECH YELLOW JACKETS
NORTH CAROLINA TAR HEELS
NC STATE WOLFPACK
NOTRE DAME FIGHTING IRISH
VIRGINIA CAVALIERS
VIRGINIA TECH HOKIES

BIG 12
BAYLOR BEARS
OKLAHOMA SOONERS
OKLAHOMA STATE COWBOYS
TCU HORNED FROGS
TEXAS LONGHORNS
TEXAS TECH RED RAIDERS
WEST VIRGINIA MOUNTAINEERS

BIG 10
MICHIGAN WOLVERINES
MICHIGAN STATE SPARTANS
NEBRASKA CORNHUSKERS
OHIO STATE BUCKEYES
PENN STATE NITTANY LIONS

SEC
ALABAMA CRIMSON TIDE
MORE ALABAMA CRIMSON TIDE
ARKANSAS RAZORBACKS
AUBURN TIGERS
MORE AUBURN TIGERS
FLORIDA GATORS
GEORGIA BULLDOGS
MORE GEORGIA BULLDOGS
KENTUCKY WILDCATS
LSU TIGERS
MISSISSIPPI STATE BULLDOGS
MISSOURI TIGERS
OLE MISS REBELS
SOUTH CAROLINA GAMECOCKS
MORE S. CAROLINA GAMECOCKS
TEXAS A&M AGGIES
TENNESSEE VOLUNTEERS

NASCAR

DAILY DEVOTIONS FOR DIE-HARD KIDS

ALABAMA CRIMSON TIDE; BAYLOR BEARS; AUBURN TIGERS;
GEORGIA BULLDOGS; LSU TIGERS; MISS. STATE BULLDOGS;
OLE MISS REBELS; TENNESSEE VOLUNTEERS;
TEXAS LONGHORNS; TEXAS A&M AGGIES

NEW STUFF

Read Colossians 3:8-10.

You have started living a new life.

Something new came to the University of Tennessee way back in 1891. It was football.

A man who had played football at Princeton was hired to start this newfangled game called football at UT. So many students showed up wanting to play that at first the school had *TWO* football teams!

The first real game was against a school called Sewanee on the Saturday after Thanksgiving in 1891. One player named Honeyman missed out on the game because a spider bit him and he had to stay in Knoxville. Only eleven players made the trip to Chattanooga; that meant the team didn't have a single sub!

Sewanee defeated the Orange and White 24-0. The *Knoxville Journal* wrote that about one hundred people went to the game. After

Volunteers

the game, the boys all got together and went to the theater to enjoy live entertainment.

Something new had come to Knoxville, and the University of Tennessee would never be the same again.

You get new stuff all the time. A new grade, new teachers, new school subjects with their new books. You may get a new brother or sister or a new place to live. You get new stuff at Christmas (hopefully not clothes).

All this pretty new stuff doesn't make a new person out of you. Inside, you're the same.

All of us have some things we would like to change about ourselves to make us better. Maybe you need to study harder. Or do your chores faster. Maybe know the Bible better.

You can be a brand new kid, changing so your life is more fun and you do what you're supposed to. A new you is possible through trusting in Jesus, who can make all things new.

Name three things you'd like to change about yourself. Start praying to Jesus, asking for his help in changing you.

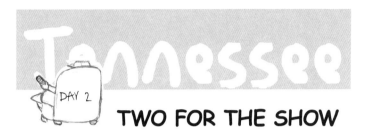

DAY 2

TWO FOR THE SHOW

Read Hebrews 12:1-3.

A huge crowd of witnesses is all around us.

To draw a crowd, a UT coach once had his team play two basketball games in one day!

John Sines coached Tennessee's men's basketball team for three seasons from 1959-62. It was not a good time for Volunteer basketball. The teams weren't very good, and they played in an old building. Not many people came to the games; even the students pretty much didn't care about UT basketball.

So Coach Sines had to come up with some wild ideas to get a crowd to a game. Perhaps his craziest notion was a doubleheader — two games for the price of one — to open the 1960-61 season. He scheduled a game against Chattanooga at 7 p.m. He then set up a second game against East Tennessee at 9.

Volunteers

That gave the players enough time to grab "a few whiffs of oxygen" and take the court.

The gimmick worked in that it drew what was then a pretty big crowd of about 2,500 folks. Led by senior guards Glenn Campbell and Bobby Carter, the Vols won both games.

You don't have a big crowd of folks cheering for you like the Vols do. No TV cameras follow you around. But you're almost always in a crowd. At school, at church, on the playground — there are people all around you.

There's another crowd all around you that you probably don't think about. That's all the folks who, like you, follow Jesus. Being a Christian isn't easy. All those grown-up Christians, the teen-aged Christians, and the kids your age who are Christians can help you.

Even when you're by yourself, you've never alone. You see, God is with you; God is part of the crowd standing by you, cheering for you.

Count each crowd you're in today or tomorrow. Remember to count God each time. What was the biggest one?

WHO, ME?

Read Judges 6:12-16.

"Lord," Gideon asked, "how can I save Israel? I'm a nobody even in my own family."

Derrick Brodus was sitting on his couch watching TV when the police showed up. They were there to take him to Neyland Stadium — to play in a game in less than an hour!

Right before the game against Middle Tennessee State in 2011, UT's kicker pulled up lame. The first-team kicker was already hurt.

Brodus was a freshman who had walked on and tried out to kick. He had never practiced with the first or second teams. He wasn't even listed on the roster. But he was the only one the worried coaches could think of.

So they called at his fraternity house where he was getting ready to watch the game on TV. This was at 6:10 p.m.; kickoff was at 7.

Volunteers

The coaches said a police car was on the way to rush him to the stadium.

So how did the surprised kicker do? He made all three of his extra points and kicked a 21-yard field goal as the Vols won 24-0. For his performance, the head coach gave him the game ball.

You ever said, "Who, me?" like Derrick Brodus did. Maybe when the teacher called on you in class? Or when somebody asked you to give a speech? Your stomach kind of knots up, doesn't it? You get real nervous, too.

That's the way Gideon felt when God called on him to lead his people in battle. And you might feel the same way when somebody calls on you to say a prayer. Or to read a part in Sunday school.

Hey, I can't do that, you might say. But you can. God wants you to do stuff for him. Like Gideon, God thinks you can do it just fine. And with God's help, you will. Just like Gideon.

Think of some ways you can help at Sunday school. And then volunteer.

PRETTY PEOPLE

Read Matthew 23:27-28.

On the outside, you are beautiful.
On the inside, you are like a tomb,
full of rotten bones.

Pat Summitt liked her players mean, not pretty. Once, though, she got busted getting pretty herself.

Summitt is a legend. From 1974-2012, she coached the Lady Vols basketball team. She won more games than any coach in college history and eight national championships.

Kristen "Ace" Clement was a guard for the 1998 undefeated national champs. She was a magician with the ball. She also, according to Summitt, was "a genuine beauty with lustrous brown hair and brown eyes."

One day, Clement showed up for practice with her hair highlighted. She told Summitt she did it because she wanted to look pretty

Volunteers

for the NCAA tournament. Summitt went nuts, saying, "We're here to look mean, not pretty."

But Summitt had a superstition: She got her hair and nails done before a big game. Sure enough, Clement showed up in her office and caught her. "Coach, we're here to look mean, not pretty," she said with a smile.

Judging people by their looks is about as silly as it comes. It doesn't tell you anything about a person. Does she use ugly words? Is he a Christian? Does he like tacos, dogs, or music? She may not even like the Vols!

Jesus said you are to look at whether people are pretty on the inside. Are they loving? Do they tell the truth? Do they love God?

This makes up the inner beauty that Jesus wants from you. Jesus isn't interested at all in whether you have hot new shoes or a pretty haircut or straight teeth. For Jesus, it's what's inside that counts.

Think of some friends. Did you use the way they looked or the way they acted to decide to be their friend?

THE SCAPEGOAT

Read Leviticus 16:20-22.

The priest put the sins of the people on the goat's head.

Austin Denny looked like the goat in the 1966 Gator Bowl. He turned out to be a hero in a Volunteer win.

As a senior tight end in '66, Denney was All-SEC and All-America. His last game at UT was against Syracuse in the Gator Bowl, so he wanted to play well.

Right off the bat, he blew it. He fumbled the opening kickoff and Syracuse recovered. "I [thought I could run] it back for a touchdown, but I forgot to take the ball," he said.

But the defense held and Tennessee led 6-0 when the head coach called for a trick play that made Denney a hero. The Vols lined up for a field goal, but it was a fake. The holder was quarterback Dewey Warren (whose nickname was the Swamp Rat). He took the snap and fired a pass into the end zone.

Denney outfought two Syracuse players to make a beautiful catch for a touchdown. The Vols went on to win 18-12.

The Bible speaks of a particular type of goat. It's called a scapegoat. It bears the blame for somebody else's sins or wrongdoing.

What a set-up! Don't clean up your room? It's that messy goat's fault. Make a bad grade on a test? The goat didn't study.

With a scapegoat, you don't have to pay for your mistakes. You get off scot-free. That's exactly the way forgiveness works with Jesus.

Your sins — the things you do that God doesn't want you to — make God unhappy with you. But Jesus steps up and says, "Daddy, I'll take the blame. I'll be the scapegoat."

God lets his own son do that because he loves you so much.

Name some things your scapegoat could take the blame for. Then ask God for forgiveness for them in Jesus' name.

YOU DECIDE

Read James 1:5-8.

*A person who doubts God can
never decide what to do.*

What a young captain decided changed the
course of Tennessee football.

In 1925, Cpt. Robert Neyland had to decide
whether to make the U.S. Army a career or do
something else with his life. For some reason,
he thought he wanted to be a football coach.

That meant he had to leave the U.S. Military
Academy. He knew of two jobs that combined
ROTC (get your dad to explain what that is) and
coaching. They were at Iowa and Tennessee.

Iowa, he decided, was mostly corn and
cows. There might actually be some people in
Tennessee. He knew, too, that football there
was pretty bad; it had nowhere to go but up.

So Cpt. Neyland decided to visit Knoxville.
He was offered a job at UT teaching military

Volunteers

science and coaching the ends. He decided to leave the army and take it.

After the season ended, Neyland became the head coach. "Real football" had begun at UT. His record was 173-31-12 in 21 seasons.

Most of the decisions in your life are made for you, aren't they? Your parents, your grand-parents, your teachers, your coaches — they decide things for you.

So when you do get the chance to make a decision, you don't want to mess it up. How can you make a good decision? It isn't always easy; sometimes deciding what to do is hard. So what do you do?

You talk it over with your parents. You pray about it with them. You look in the Bible with them to see if God has a word about the choice you face. When you know what God's answer is, you do it. When you obey God, you can know that you are doing the right thing.

Make a list of the decisions you will make tomorrow. Go ahead and pray for God's help in making them.

DAY 7

FOOD FIGHT

Read Genesis 9:1-3.

*I now give you everything that lives
and moves to eat.*

Growing up, Antone Davis never knew from one day to another if he would have enough food to eat.

Davis once said, "Manners were not at the top of my list. Football was not at the top of my list. Survival was at the top of my list." Survival meant food.

As a senior, he went to a military school. For the first time in his life, he didn't have to worry about food. So he ate — a lot.

When Davis was recruited by major schools, he continued to wolf down the food. He committed to Tennessee but took a trip to South Carolina just for the fun of it. And for the food. He said he "ate everything he [could] under the sun."

Volunteers

The result was a whole bunch of pounds. He arrived in Knoxville in 1987 tipping the scales at 349 pounds. Line coach Phillip Fulmer told him he had to get down to 300 pounds.

Two months later, he had done it. As a senior in 1990, he was named the SEC's best blocker.

Americans really do love food. We love to eat all sorts of different things, from hamburgers to chicken, pizza to ice cream. We even have TV channels that talk about food all the time. They show people how to make new dishes for their family to try and eat.

Food is one of God's really good ideas. Isn't it amazing to think that from one apple seed, an entire tree full of apples can grow and give you yummy fruit year after year?

God created this system that lets all living things grow and nourish one another. Your food comes from God and nowhere else. The least you can do is thank him for it.

Three questions to answer: What's your favorite food? What can you cook? Do you always thank God before you eat?

DAY 8

WHAT'S YOUR EXCUSE?

Read Luke 9:59-62.

If you start to follow Jesus and then make excuses not to serve him, you are not fit for Heaven.

One of UT's greatest kickers made it in the pros because he didn't make excuses.

From 1981-84, Fuad Reveiz was All-SEC three times and set all kinds of records.

His coach was Vol legend George Cafego. He knew nothing about Hispanic names, so he asked Reveiz, who is from Colombia, how to pronounce his name. That didn't help. "I'm not going to learn Latin," the coach said. "Your name is Frank."

For four years, Cafego barked, "Frank, let's go" when kicking time came. Until Reveiz' last home game. That time, he said, "Fuad, go kick it." "I had earned his respect," Reveiz said.

He was drafted by the Miami Dolphins, who

had a kicker on hand. "He never missed a field goal in his life," Reveiz said. He meant the kicker always had an excuse, something Cafego had coached him never to do.

Reveiz got the job. The Dolphins head coach told him he couldn't stand excuse-making.

You've made some excuses before, haven't you? What excuse did you use when you didn't do your homework? Or didn't do your chores? Have you ever said you felt bad so you didn't have to do something you didn't want to?

Lots of folks make excuses when we don't like the way things are going. Or when stuff gets too hard. Or we fail at something.

We do it with our faith life, too. We say the Bible's too hard to read. The weather's too pretty to be shut up in church. Or praying in public is downright embarrassing.

But, you know, Jesus died for you without making any excuses. The least you can do is live for him with no excuses.

What excuse did you use the last time you missed church? Do you think God thought it was a good one?

DAY 9

ALL IN

Read Mark 12:28-31.

"Love the Lord your God with all your heart, all your soul, all your mind, and all your strength."

Any doctor will tell you: You can't play football on a torn ACL. (The ACL is one of four ligaments that hold the knee together.) But thanks to his faith and his love of Tennessee football, Jacob Gilliam did.

Gilliam began the 2014 football season at left tackle but tore his ACL in the first game. He called his dad in tears, saying his career was over. His dad disagreed, saying Jacob's mom and he were coming to Knoxville to pray for God to heal him.

They did just that, laying hands on their son's injured knee and praying for a miracle.

Gilliam decided not to have surgery. Doctors said if he played, he would make it worse. He

Volunteers

answered, "I believe I'm protected [by God]. Nothing's going to happen to me."

It didn't. Forty-nine days after the injury that should have ended his career, Gilliam started against Alabama. He started in every game the rest of the season.

Jacob Gilliam was all in for Tennessee.

What is it that you really like so much that you'd do it all the time if you could? It's called having "zeal" or "enthusiasm" for something. For instance, do you jump up and down and whoop and holler when the Vols score?

What about your zeal for the Lord? On Sunday morning, if you go to church at all, do you pretty much act like you're getting your teeth cleaned or are about to get a shot?

Jesus made it clear which rule is number one to God. You are to be all in for God, to love him with all your heart, all your soul, all your mind, all your strength.

You should be fired up for God! Are you?

Promise God that at church Sunday you will sing real loud and will listen to the sermon and not talk all through it.

SNAKES ALIVE!

Read Matthew 23:29-34.

You snakes! You bunch of vipers!

Tennessee coaches ran into snakes and bats when they recruited one player.

Guard Bill Mayo was a four-year starter for the Volunteers from 1981-84. As a senior, he was All-America and All-SEC, blocking for running back Johnny Jones, who ran for 1,290 yards.

To recruit Mayo, line coach Phillip Fulmer (who later would be the head coach) let Mayo take him caving. Mayo said Fulmer did all right "for the first hour or two." A former offensive lineman, Fulmer didn't exactly have the body shape to be in a cave. He had trouble with some tight spots and even had to crawl on his stomach a time or two to keep going.

But he did all right until he stopped one time and put a hand on a wall to steady himself.

"He put his hand on a bat," Mayo said.

Head coach Johnny Majors decided that he needed to visit Mayo's home to make sure he was coming to Knoxville. The visit went well until Mayo pulled out his pet: an eight-foot-long python. Majors said he tried to be polite, but "I didn't want much to do with that snake."

When you think about snakes, you probably don't get happy thoughts. In the Bible, snakes are used as a symbol for something or some-one who is really bad.

Jesus used the word "snake" to describe the Pharisees. They were Jewish religious leaders who looked and acted nice and faithful on the outside. On the inside, though, they were mean and did not love Jesus.

Being true to your faith, being kind to others, and loving Jesus will keep Jesus from thinking that you are like a snake.

Act out what you would do if you found a big snake in your room. Then act out what you would do if you found a person who didn't love Jesus in your room.

AT HOME

Read 2 Corinthians 5:6-9.

*We would really rather be out of
our bodies and at home with God.*

Because of a really old rule about what a team could wear at home, the Lady Vol basketball team plays its home games in uniforms different from every other Tennessee team.

Women's basketball began at Tennessee in 1968. There were no scholarships. A good crowd was twenty people. When the first coach took over, the team didn't even have any uniforms. Players wore T-shirts and shorts.

Companies that made women's uniforms didn't offer orange ones back then. The coach used white with orange letters for road games.

But a rule said home teams couldn't wear white. The coach had to find some other color for home games. She liked Carolina blue, and she could get it.

Soon, orange uniforms could be found. But the next time you see the Lady Vols play at home check out their unis. You'll see a touch of Carolina blue, a tradition from the old days.

When somebody says "home," what do you think about? A house? Your room? Your toys?

But home isn't just a place. More than walls and floors, a home is about people. You are at home when you are with the people you love and the people who love you. That's why it doesn't matter what you live in. What matters is the people you share it with, including God.

Oddly, as a Christian, you spend your whole life as a kid and as a grown-up away from your real home. That's because your real home is with God and Jesus in Heaven. There you will live forever with the people whom you love and who love you most of all.

You'll be home because you'll be with God, and nobody loves you more than God does.

List the different places you have lived. What was different about each one? What made them all feel like home?

STRANGE BUT TRUE

Read Philippians 2:5-11.

Jesus is God, but he became a servant and died on a cross.

It's strange but true: Tennessee once had a player get kicked out of a football game twice and another player who got kicked out but wouldn't leave.

The Vols of 1950 went 11-1, but had to hold Washington & Lee inside the 5-yard line in the last minute to win 27-20.

During that goal-line stand, a fight broke out. A ref kicked UT's Gordon Polofsky out of the game. But more commotion broke out before the ref could take Polofsky to the sideline. So he went to the back of the crowd and tried to hide among the other players. The ref spotted him, though, and ordered Polofsky to take a seat on the bench — for a second time.

The cause of the ruckus was UT end Doug

Atkins, who also had been kicked out of the game. He refused to leave the field.

A huge man, Atkins didn't do much of anything he didn't want to. The ref finally went to the Tennessee head coach and asked for help. The coach told him, "YOU kicked him out. YOU get him off the field."

A lot of things about life are strange. Isn't it strange that you can't eat all the sugar you want to? Isn't it strange that you can't play all the time when everybody knows that's what kids are good at?

God's kind of strange, too, isn't he? He's the ruler of all the universe; he can do anything he wants to. And so he let himself be killed by a bunch of men who nailed him to two pieces of wood. Isn't that downright weird?

And why did God do it? That's strange, too. He did it because he loves you so much. In the person of Jesus, God died so you can be his friend.

List five things about God that are strange (like he knows everything). Tell why they're strange.

A LONG SHOT

Read Matthew 9:9-10.

*Jesus said, "Follow me," and
Matthew got up and did it.*

Polio. Rheumatic fever. Quit the team. Got kicked off it another time. And this guy would be a star? Talk about your long shot.

When he was 9, Frank Emanuel came down with rheumatic fever. At 10, he had polio. But this long shot who didn't even start school until he was 8 was a high-school football star.

When he got to Knoxville, he was so homesick he decided to give up football and get a job. He walked into his home and found two UT coaches waiting for him. They talked him into coming back.

Then Emanuel got into a big brawl and was kicked off the team. He wound up sleeping under the stadium. Teammates sneaked him food from the dining hall.

Volunteers

The head coach gave this long shot a second chance. In 1965, he was an All-American linebacker. Frank Emanuel was later elected to the College Football Hall of Fame.

A long shot is someone or some team that doesn't stand a good chance of doing something. You're a pretty long shot to get married this year or to be named a coach at Tennessee.

Matthew was a long shot to become one of Jesus' close friends. He was a tax collector, which meant he was pretty much a crook. He got rich by bullying and stealing from his own people, his own neighbors.

Yet, Jesus said only two words to this lowlife: "Follow me." And Matthew did it.

Like Matthew, we're all long shots to get to Heaven because we can't stand before God with pure, clean hearts. Not unless we do what Matthew did: Get up and follow Jesus. Then we become a sure thing.

Name five things that are long shots in your life (like becoming president). Then name five things that are sure shots (like going to bed tonight).

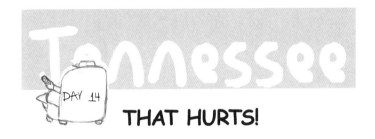

THAT HURTS!

Read 2 Corinthians 1:3-7.

*God is the father of all comfort in
our pain and our suffering.*

Bridgette Gordon could play with pain.

Gordon is a Lady Vol legend. In 1990, her
jersey number 30 was retired. From 1985-89,
she led the team to four straight Final Fours
and two national championships.

On April 2, 1989, she wasn't having a good
night, against Auburn in the national championship game. Head coach Pat Summitt called
timeout to give her a good talking-to.

Gordon only half-listened. She stood with
her hand over her mouth. So Summitt got
right in her face. The coach barked at Gordon
to "get back in there and do something."

Gordon nodded and did what her coach said.
She went out and sank three straight shots
and finished the game with 27 points. Ten-

nessee won its second national title.

After the game, Summitt learned that right before she had jumped all over Gordon, her star had taken an elbow to the face. The shot was so hard it knocked a tooth loose. She had to have a root canal to save it.

Does a day go by when you don't feel pain? A scrape from a fall on the playground. A blister from your shoes. A bump on the head.

Some pain isn't just physical like that blow Bridgett Gordon got. Bruises and bumps don't hurt nearly as bad as it does when your dog dies or someone is mean to you.

Jesus knows all about pain. After all, they drove nails into his hands and feet, hung him on two pieces of wood, and stuck a spear in his side. It was an awful, painful way to die.

So when you hurt, you can find comfort in Jesus. He's been there before. He knows all about tears and pain.

Look over your body for bumps, bruises, scratches, and scrapes. Tell how you got each one and how bad it hurt.

MIRACLE PLAY

Read Matthew 12:38-40.

Jesus said, "Wicked and unfaithful people ask for miracles" to convince them he is Lord and Savior.

George Cafego always called it a miracle that UT head football coach Bob Neyland showed up in 1936 to watch him play.

That's because Cafego lived in what he called a "near-nothing" town in West Virginia. The only future he had was living and dying in the coal mines. But Neyland told him "I'll take care of you." He meant a football scholarship.

Cafego had nothing, not even a home. Both his parents were dead. He lived with his high-school coaches and with miners in a boarding house. He often just slept on any floor space he could find.

He had six dollars and a borrowed suitcase held together with string when he got to Knoxville. He had no sheets or blankets because he couldn't afford them.

He had to wear a suit to away games, so the coaches took him to town and bought him the first suit and tie he ever owned.

He paid them back. Cafego was an All-American running back who was elected to the Hall of Fame. He coached at UT for thirty years.

A miracle is something that you can't explain except by saying God did it. Some people say miracles are rare, but they are wrong.

Since God made the world and everything in it, the whole world is a miracle. You are a miracle! Just think: There's nobody else in the world like you. You're so special God made only one of you (unless you're a twin!).

A lot of people don't see miracles around them because they don't have any faith in God. Jesus knew that seeing a miracle doesn't make someone believe in him. But since you believe in Jesus and God, you can see miracles.

List some things around you that are miracles because God made them.

THE GREATEST

Read Mark 9:33-37.

*To be the greatest in God's
kingdom, you must put others
above yourself and serve them.*

Vol head coach Johnny Majors called it the greatest game any team of his had ever played.

It was the 1980 Auburn game. The largest crowd ever to watch a game in Auburn saw their team get the daylights beat out of it. Tennessee slaughtered the Tigers 42-0. It was the worst beating at home the school had ever taken.

With a 1-2 record, Tennessee went into the game as the underdog. Auburn was favored.

Right before the game, Majors named Jeff Olszewski as the starting quarterback. He hit the field throwing and never stopped. At one point, he completed 11 straight passes.

The running game was just as good. James

Berry scored three touchdowns. The defense forced six turnovers.

The Vols led 28-0 at halftime. Auburn's head coach said he felt like "General Custer among all these Indians."

It was indeed one of UT's greatest games.

When you think about being the greatest at something, what do you think of? Probably being better than everybody else, right? You get the highest score on a video game or on a test. You win at tennis. You build the greatest thing of all with your Legos.

But Jesus turned being the greatest upside down. He said something really strange. To be the greatest for Jesus, you have to be last. How weird is that? What he meant is that you must put other people first in your life. You always are kind to and help other people.

If you live like that, God is so pleased with you that he names you one of his children. You can't be any greater than that!

To be the greatest, find somebody at school to smile at them and help them.

HUGS AND KISSES

Read John 15:9-14.

Jesus said, "I have loved you. Now remain in my love."

Sarah Wyche had one big special hug for her quarterback son, Bubba.

Only Tennessee stayed with Bubba Wyche when he tore his knee up before his senior year of high school. But at UT, injuries limited him to only six passes his first three seasons.

In 1967, he got into the Ga. Tech game after the first two quarterbacks got hurt. UT won 24-13, and he was named the Southeastern Back of the Week.

Since Wyche had seen no chance of playing, he had sold his Tech tickets for a little pocket money. Thus, his parents missed the game. His mother wasn't going to miss the next one.

It was Alabama, which had won 26 games in a row. Bubba's momma didn't have a ticket,

Volunteers

but she went to Birmingham anyhow. She walked from gate to gate, trying to get in. She finally told a gatekeeper, "My boy's starting at quarterback for Tennessee. I've got to get in."

He let her in, telling her she would have to stand up. She did, and she saw it all. Her son led the Vols to a 24-13 defeat of Alabama. When the game was over, she found Bubba and gave him one of her biggest hugs ever.

A hug is a sign of affection. When you hug someone, you're showing them you care for them. It doesn't just make them feel good; it makes you feel good, too. A hug is also a symbol. When you hold someone close, it says how closely you hold them in your heart.

The greatest hugger of them all is God. Through Jesus, God tries to pull us closer to him because he loves us. A good hug takes two, so God always wants us to hug him back.

We do that by loving Jesus. To love Jesus is to hug God — and that feels mighty good.

Think of some folks you'd like to hug and then do it when you see them.

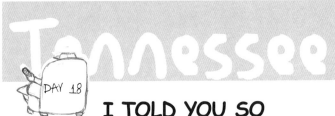
I TOLD YOU SO

Read Matthew 24:30-35.

Jesus will come on the clouds in power and glory.

Michael Palardy did what he told head coach Butch Jones he would do, and Tennessee won.

In 2013, the underdog Vols hosted 11th-ranked South Carolina. They led 17-7 at half-time, but the Gamecocks came flying back to lead 21-17 in the third quarter. Palardy kicked a field goal to make it a one-point game.

With about three minutes left, South Carolina punted. The Vols had one last chance. They made the most of it.

Freshman Marquez North caught a 39-yard pass, and junior Marlin Lane ran the ball four straight times. UT sat on the Carolina 2-yard line with only seconds left on the clock.

On the day before the game, Coach Jones had said to Palardy, "You've got the game

Volunteers

winner tomorrow, right?" The kicker replied, "I got you, Coach."

So now Jones told Palardy to do what he had said he would. He did. As time ran out, he booted a 19-yard field goal. 23-21, Tennessee.

One day Jesus is going to come back and find everyone who has been faithful to him. He will gather them all up and take them to Heaven. There they will live with God forever in happiness and love. It will be the most glorious time ever.

How do we know that's going to happen? Jesus told us so. When will it happen? Well, he didn't tell us that. He just told us to be ready so we don't miss it.

How do you get ready? It's simple. You just love Jesus. You live your life for Jesus. You remember that Jesus is counting on you, and you do everything for him.

Are you ready?

***Put some ice cream in a bowl
and watch it melt to remind you
that Jesus may come back at any time,
maybe even before the ice cream melts.***

PIONEER SPIRIT

Read Luke 5:4-11.

They pulled their boats on shore and left everything to follow Jesus.

Coach and I never talked about it, Larry Robinson said. "It" had to do with the fact that Robinson was a pioneer; he was doing something that had never been done before.

In 1971, Robinson became the first African-American player in the history of UT basketball. He was called "the perfect man for his time and his pioneering situation." He was one of 15 children raised in a Christian home. He was such a good athlete that the UT football coach offered him a scholarship.

Robinson wasn't the only black athlete on campus; the football team had been integrated in 1968. (Talk with an adult about integration.) To Tennessee's credit, race just never became an issue. "He was accepted wholeheartedly,"

Volunteers

said a fellow athlete.

It helped that he was a good player. As a senior in 1972-73, Robinson was again a pioneer: He was named team captain. He scored 11.7 points a game to lead the Volunteers to a second-place finish in the SEC.

A pioneer is a person, like Larry Robinson, who is the first person to do something or to try something no one else has done before. The disciples who gave up fishing to follow Jesus were pioneers.

Being a pioneer is scary, but it's also fun. Learning something new in school, going to a new place on vacation, riding a new ride at the fair — it's exciting!

God wants you to go to new places and to try new things for him. He wants you to follow him no matter what. After a while, you get really good at being a Christian and then you can help others become pioneers for Jesus.

Talk with a parent or grandparent about how brave Larry Robinson was and why he had to be that way.

THE INTERVIEW

Read Romans 14:9-12.

We will all have to explain to God everything we have done.

Heath Shuler's first interview for college scouts took place on the football field. It didn't go like everybody wanted it to.

In 1993, Shuler was the SEC Player of the Year. The Vols went 9-2-1 as he threw 25 touchdown passes. He was the runner-up for the Heisman Trophy.

Shuler played for a small high school in North Carolina, so a lot of folks didn't hear about him. The first game of his senior year was the first time most college coaches saw him play in person. It didn't quite work out.

First of all, it rained. In the confusion, Shuler forgot his game pants! He had to borrow some from a reserve.

Then the other team decided they wouldn't

let Shuler beat them. They used ten backs to keep him from throwing! So he didn't throw. He just kept tucking the ball away and running.

All the college scouts that showed up didn't get to see what they had come for.

When grown-ups get famous or want a job, they have an interview. They answer questions from people.

You'll probably have a job interview one day. Sooner than that, you may have an interview at a pageant or to get into a school club.

Interviews are hard because people ask you questions and judge you. That means they decide whether you are good enough for what they want. Nobody likes to be judged.

One day, you will show up in Heaven. The Bible tells us that we all will be judged by God. You will have an interview with God.

Talk about being nervous! How in the world can you be good enough for God? All it takes is Jesus. Jesus makes you good enough.

Pretend you're being interviewed by God. What would you tell him about yourself?

WAIT UP!

Read Acts 1:1-4.

Wait for the gift my Father promised.

The Vols got a lesson in waiting when they played Ole Miss in 2004.

Thanks to TV, the game in Mississippi didn't start until 8 p.m., which was 9 p.m. Knoxville time. "When people are going to bed, we'll still be playing," said punter Dustin Colquitt.

The coaches and players had a lot of time to kill. "I hate the late start. The day takes forever," said assistant coach Trooper Taylor. "You sit there looking at the clock all day."

Lineman Rob Smith solved the problem by doing a lot of sleeping. "I'm a big sleeper," he said. "I sleep all day when we're not meeting."

Many of the players watched football on TV. Not Colquitt. He never watched football before a game after he saw a punt get blocked. "I

Volunteers

just don't want to see that stuff," he said.

Once the wait was over, the Vols whipped the Rebels 21-17. They would make it to the SEC title game and the Cotton Bowl.

The wait turned out to be worth it.

Sitting around and waiting is just plain old awful. A doctor's or dentist's office is the worst of all. How about waiting for Christmas or your birthday to get here?

Most people don't like to wait on God either. Have you ever prayed for something? You probably wanted it right away, didn't you? Then did you get upset with God when you had to wait?

But Jesus' last command to his disciples was to wait. One day Jesus will return, but right now we all have to wait for it. That goes for you, too. While you wait on God, you go to church, read the Bible, and trust in God. You grow stronger in your faith.

Waiting for God is never time lost.

Practice waiting by sitting in a chair and telling your favorite Bible story out loud.

BELIEVE IT OR NOT

Read Hebrews 3:12-14.

Do not have an unbelieving heart that turns you away from God.

What UGA did to Tennessee was hard to believe. But what the Vols did to the Dawgs six seconds later was unbelievable.

On Oct. 1, 2016, the two old foes played one of the most unbelievable games in college football history. With only ten seconds left to play, Georgia threw a 47-yard touchdown pass to give the Bulldogs a 31-28 lead.

The game was over. Well, maybe not.

"There was no panic," UT head coach Butch Jones said. "I looked the kids in the eyes and said we were going to find a way."

Unbelievably, they did.

The kickoff return and a penalty left UT at the Bulldog 43 with four seconds left. Quarterback Joshua Dobbs threw what Jones called "the best ball of his career" into a crowd in the end zone. Receiver Jauan Jennings came down with the ball for an unbelievable score.

Jones sank to his knees in joy. Back Alvin Kamara fell onto his back in disbelief.

Tennessee unbelievably had a 34-31 win.

You know, it doesn't really matter if you don't believe in some things. Like magic. That walking under a ladder can bring you bad luck. Or that touching frogs can give you warts.

But it matters a whole lot that you believe in Jesus as the Son of God. Some people say that Jesus was a good man and a good teacher and that's all.

They are wrong, and their unbelief is bad for them. God doesn't fool around with people who don't believe in Jesus as their Savior. He locks them out of Heaven forever.

Believing in Jesus is about the way you live now and the way you will live forever.

Talk to your parents about some things you don't believe in and some things you do believe in and why.

I KNOW THAT!

Read John 4:25-26, 39-42.

"We know that this man really is the Savior of the world."

The Vol defense knew something. So they pulled off one of UT's most famous plays and saved a big upset.

The Volunteers of 1959 were big underdogs when LSU rolled into town. The Tigers were undefeated and were ranked No. 1.

LSU led 7-0 in the third quarter, but the UT defense scored twice for a 14-7 lead. LSU scored with 13:44 to play. The Tigers decided to go for two points to take the lead.

At that time, the two-point conversion was so new that Tennessee had never tried one or tried to stop one. But everyone on the defense knew who would get the ball.

That would be Billy Cannon, LSU's running back who had won the Heisman Trophy the year before. He would get the ball, but where would he go?

The Vols had watched films. They knew that Cannon moved back a little when he was running to his right. He did that, so they knew what was coming. The defense was there to pull off what became known as "The Stop."

Tennessee won 14-13.

The defense knew that wonderful day against LSU the same way you know some things in your life. You know what your favorite subject is in school (lunch?) and what your favorite ice cream flavor is. You know you're a UT fan.

Nobody can work it out on paper why you know these things. You just do. That's the way it is with your faith in Jesus. You know that he is God's son and is the savior of the world. You know it with all your heart and soul.

You just know it, and because you know him, Jesus knows you. That is all you really need to know.

List ten things you know for sure about yourself and your life. Shouldn't #1 be "I am a Christian"?

DAY 24

DEAD WRONG

Read Matthew 26:14-16; 27:1-5.

*Judas was ashamed and sad
because he had betrayed Jesus.*

Coaches said he wasn't good enough, that he couldn't play offense or defense. Boy, were they wrong.

Tim Irwin wanted to play for Notre Dame. The head coach saw some of his films and told him he wasn't good enough to play major college ball anywhere, especially Notre Dame.

Tennessee recruited him, and he arrived in Knoxville in 1977. At a coaches' meeting one day, his name came up. A UT coach said Irwin couldn't play defense or offense for the Vols. He wasn't good enough.

Irwin knew that he wasn't the best athlete around, but "I knew I could try and outwork everybody else." Coach Tim Dyer spent extra time with him, and they became good friends.

Volunteers

Irwin's hard work paid off. He was a starter in 1978. In 1979, the Vols blasted Notre Dame 40-18. A Notre Dame lineman said, Irwin "is as good as anybody I will see all year."

Irwin made All-SEC in 1980 and had a 14-year career in the NFL. He had done what he set out to do: prove all those coaches wrong.

Everybody's wrong at some time or other. Maybe you walked into the wrong classroom at school. How many times have you come up with the wrong answer on a test?

Here's a secret: Even grown-ups are wrong.

Think about Judas. He turned Jesus over to folks who wanted to kill him. Can anything be more wrong than that?

Judas felt sorry about what he did to Jesus, but it didn't help. That's because he tried to make it all right himself instead of asking God to forgive him. He was dead wrong this time.

When you do something wrong, you make it worse if you don't pray to God for forgiveness.

***Think of something you did wrong today.
Ask God to forgive you. How do you feel?***

THINGS CHANGE

Read Hebrews 13:5-8.

*Jesus Christ is the same yesterday
and today and forever.*

What kind of crazy game was this?

The ball was shaped like a watermelon! Players could barely hold it and couldn't throw it. Fans ran onto the field in the middle of the game and got in the way of the players. Players had long hair for protection because they didn't wear helmets.

There were no scoreboards. The fields didn't have lights so the teams couldn't play after dark. The halves were as long as what the players wanted them to be. Sometimes they played until they got tired and decided to stop.

Teammates dragged the guy with the ball forward. Some players had handles sewn into their pants to make it easier to toss them down the field. In one game, a player hid on

Volunteers

the sidelines in street clothes; that means he didn't have a uniform on. When the play started, he stepped onto the field and caught a pass.

What silly game was that? Believe it or not, it was college football back in the early days. Football has sure changed, hasn't it?

Just like football at Tennessee, the world around you is always changing. You might get a new teacher or move to a new school. Your parents may get a new car for the family. You may even get a new brother or sister!

You change, too. Your feet get bigger so you get new shoes. You may have grown an inch or two since last summer so you need new shirts and new jeans or skirts.

Even though lots of things change around you, there is one thing that doesn't change: Jesus. Jesus is the same all the time.

Jesus loves you always and his love for you never changes. No matter what.

What has changed in your life recently? Did you like it or did it scare you?

FIGHT NIGHT

Read Hebrews 12:14-15.

Do all you can to live in peace with everyone.

While he was at UT, Steve Kiner was not exactly a peace-loving man.

Kiner is a Tennessee legend. A linebacker, he was All-America in 1968 and '69. He was elected to the College Football Hall of Fame in 1999.

He never stepped away from a fight. One time at practice, a player tried to block him at his knees. Kiner lifted up the player's helmet and popped him in the nose. The player went to the locker room and came back with two knives. He told Kiner he was going to cut his throat. Kiner warned him he better stop. When he didn't, Kiner calmly clobbered him.

One night at dinner, a big basketball player told Kiner he had to move. "I thought he was joking," Kiner said, "but he wasn't." He pushed Kiner, who slugged him, picked him up, and slammed him onto a table. End of fight.

As one Volunteer coach put it, "It wasn't a good idea to take on Kiner."

To his credit, Kiner went on to earn three degrees and become a mental health therapist.

Have you ever played in a game of some kind where a player from the other team hurt you? Maybe you wanted to fight because of it.

No matter what happens, no matter where you are, no matter what someone else has done to you — fighting is never the answer. It's not just because you make an enemy but also because Jesus said you should make peace and make a friend instead of fighting.

Trying to make peace isn't as easy as taking a swing or saying ugly things to someone. It does requires more courage. It's also exactly what Jesus would do.

Try talking to a person at school you don't get along with and making him or her your friend.

CROWD CONTROL

Read Matthew 27:15-17, 20-24.

*The crowd was getting mad, so
Pilate handed Jesus over to them
to be crucified.*

At one Tennessee-Alabama game, the crowd kept getting in the way of the players!

In 1901, the teams met in Birmingham, but they had a big problem. The crowd wouldn't stay off the field. After almost every play, spectators would run out and form a ring around the players. That meant the teams couldn't run a play.

Some local policemen tried hard to keep the mob off the field, but they couldn't. Over and over, the refs had to take long timeouts to shoo the crowd off the field so the players had enough room to run a play.

Ten minutes into the last half, the teams got into a dispute over an offside call against

Alabama. Most of the crowd rushed onto the field to find out what was going on and to put their two cents worth in.

All those delays made the game so long that it began to get dark. The refs had to call the game with the score tied at six.

One of the most difficult parts of growing up is learning not to go along with whatever a crowd of your friends decides to do when you know it is wrong.

A bunch of folks may want to do something, but that doesn't make it right. You have to listen to your own inner voice, your conscience to decide. It's the voice of the Holy Spirit telling you what to do.

If you follow Jesus, everything else in your life — including your friends — stands behind him. Unlike Pontius Pilate, you never go along with what the crowd says to do; you go along with what Jesus says you should do.

Talk about a time at school when some friends did something wrong. Did you go along with them? Why or why not?

TICK TOCK

Matthew 25:1-13.

*Stay alert. You don't know the day
or the hour when Jesus will return.*

Before there was a shot clock in college basketball, the Vols played the lowest scoring game in modern history.

During the 1973-74 season, UT scored 96 points in a win over DePaul. The next night — get this now — Tennessee beat Temple 11-6. Seventeen total points! Neither team made a field goal the last half!

The Temple coach knew his boys couldn't run with the Vols. So he told his team to hold the ball as long as they could. Tennessee coach Ray Mears told his team to stay under the goal in a zone defense.

The result was a standoff; all the players just stood around. At one point in the first half, Temple held the ball while almost 13 minutes ticked off the clock! The last half was more of the same with only a few free throws made. Annoyed UT fans pelted the court with ice, but neither team would move.

After the game, Coach Mears brought his team back out for a scrimmage so the fans at least had something to watch.

Even though you're a kid, the clock has a lot to do with your life. You have to be at school on time or you're headed for big trouble. Athletic events, classes, church, even birthday parties — they all start at a certain time. You probably have a bedtime on school nights.

All that time, every second of your life, is a gift from God since he's the one who dreamed up time in the first place.

So what does God consider making good use of the time he gives us? As Jesus' story tells us, it's being ready for the wonderful and glorious day when Jesus will return.

When will that be? Only time will tell.

Count to sixty but not real fast.
That's a minute. Any minute now
Jesus could come back.

BAD WEATHER

Read Nahum 1:3-5.

God alone controls the wind and the storms.

Just how cold was it for the 1950 Kentucky game? Tennessee center Bob Davis was injured; every time he spit blood, it would hit his face guard and turn into an icicle!

"It makes me cold to think about it," Davis said almost fifty years after that game. Two days before the game, the skies had been clear and sunny. That night, though, a storm moved in. It brought six inches of snow and 13-degree temperatures.

Some UT fraternity boys shoveled the snow off the tarp on the field, but the tarp was so frozen they had to chop it up. There weren't enough people to clean off the seats, so the fans had to sit in snow and shiver.

Davis had his nose broken in the first half.

Volunteers

As the center, every time he leaned over the ball, blood dripped onto it. All-American running back Hank Lauricella complained about that. So Davis wore a face guard for the only time in his career. Thus, icicles.

Nobody could hold onto the ball. Kentucky fumbled eight times while the Vols lost seven fumbles. Davis got one of the UK fumbles that set up a TD that was the game's only score.

You can look out a window and see a storm coming, but you can't stop it, can you? You can do a lot of things, but only God controls the weather.

God has so much power you can't imagine it. But you also can't imagine how much God loves you. He loves you so much that as Jesus he died in pain on a nasty cross for you.

God is so powerful that he can make it rain and can push the clouds around. The weather does what he tells it to. But the strongest thing of all about God is his love for you.

List all the kinds of bad weather you can think of. Tell a parent what you'd do in case of each one.

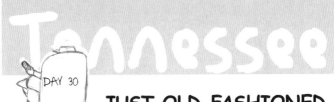

JUST OLD-FASHIONED

Read Leviticus 18:1-5.

*You must obey my laws. I am the
Lord your God.*

A long time ago, women at UT had to go to
PE so they could build up their weak ankles
and little lungs. Kinda old-fashioned, huh?

Think about the female athletes at Tennessee today. We cheer for them as they dazzle
us with their grace and ability. Back in 1899,
though, women were seen as weak and had
to be taken care of for their own good. No way
they could play sports that were tough like
softball and soccer. They might get hurt! They
could do croquet, archery, and tennis.

So it's strange that the women had a basketball team early on. Then in 1920, the university granted women students permission
to have varsity track, swimming, and tennis
teams.

Volunteers

That didn't last very long. UT educators soon used old-fashioned ideas about women to put an end to contests against other colleges. UT didn't have any women's intercollegiate sports again until a volleyball tournament in 1959.

Phones used to sit in one place in the house with a wire running from them. You had to dial the numbers one at a time. Cars didn't have automatic transmissions; you had to shift the gears yourself. (Cars had three pedals, but we only have two feet. How did that work?)

Some old-fashioned things aren't around anymore, and we're glad for it. But not all old things are bad. Old-fashioned ice cream is still the best. So is old-fashioned root beer.

And so are God's laws that tell you how to live. They are thousands of years old, but they still work. They still lead you to a happy life. How can you know about them? They're in your Bible, which is God's book.

Doing what God says is never old-fashioned.

Talk to a grandparent about how things were when he/she was your age.

BODY LANGUAGE

Read 1 Corinthians 6:19-20.

Honor God with your body.

He didn't look much like a football player, but he sure was one.

Herman Hickman was round. He was 5-10 and weighed 213 lbs. when he played for the Vols in the 1920s and early '30s. As an adult, his weight ballooned to 330 lbs. He once said, "I can usually tell after the first steak or two if a dinner is going to be [any good]."

Despite his unusual body shape and size, Hickman was a great player. A guard, he was both All-America and All-Pro.

The Vols played a charity game against New York University in 1931. Tennessee won 13-0. The NYU coach asked a player "if the little fat man from Tennessee was all that tough." The player said, "I'll tell you how tough he was. He kept calling me a Yankee and I pretended I didn't hear him."

The strangest thing Hickman ever ate was a page from *Sports Illustrated*. He wrote that Ga. Tech would beat Tennessee, and the Vols won. He literally ate his words.

Have you ever compared yourself to others and what they look like? Maybe you have a friend who's taller than you are. Or who has blond hair you wish you had. You start looking in the mirror and wishing you looked different.

That's the danger of comparing yourself to other people like your friends or TV or movie stars. Someone always looks the way that you wish you did. So you start feeling sad about yourself and the way you look.

But here's a truth to remember: Others wish they looked like you. Even God likes the way you look. After all, he made you that way.

And remember. You're so special to God that he lives with you as the Holy Spirit. Your body is God's home.

Look closely at yourself in the mirror.
Look for features that you like.
Then thank God for them.

DAY 32

FACING THE MUSIC

Read Psalm 98:4-6.

*Shout to the Lord, burst into song,
and make music.*

Come on, Dewey, hum that tater." That's the song The Swamp Rat had his linemen singing.

Dewey Warren grew up in the marshes around Savannah, Ga. He was late for practice one day, and his coach said he was just like an old swamp rat. The nickname stuck.

A quarterback, Warren got into his first UT game in 1965 when the starter was injured. He trotted into the huddle and everybody started laughing. He didn't have his helmet!

The Swamp Rat was UT's first pure passing quarterback. He was limping after one game, and a coach asked him if he could play next week. Warren said, "As long as I can stand on one leg and raise my right arm, Old Dewey will be humming that tater."

His offensive linemen picked up on what he said and set it to music. They soon had a song they sang in the huddle: "Come on, Dewey, hum that tater."

Dewey hummed that tater. He ended up in 1967 holding practically every passing record in the Volunteer books.

Can you sing without having everyone run from the room holding their ears? Maybe you can play the guitar, the piano, or the drums.

If you like music, then you have music in your heart. But do you ever let that music come out in praise of God the way it comes out in praise of the Vols? Do you sing in church, or do you just kind of stand there and mumble a few words? Are you embarrassed to sing?

Music and singing have almost always been a part of worshipping God. Think about this: God loves you and he always will. That should make you sing for joy, especially in church.

Sing "Rocky Top" and your favorite church song. Remember that God likes to hear you sing praises to him.

KEEP OUT!

Read Exodus 26:30-34.

The curtain will separate the Holy Room from the Most Holy Room.

A UT basketball legend first played the game because he wanted to belong.

Ernie Grunfeld finished at UT after the 1977 season as the school's all-time leading scorer. He teamed with Bernard King to form the "Ernie and Bernie Show" at Tennessee. His jersey number 22 was retired in 2008.

His family fled Romania and religious persecution when Ernie was 9. They settled in a New York City suburb, and he was happy about it. But Ernie was a Jewish kid from Eastern Europe. He had to find some way to fit in. That way turned out to be basketball.

He went out to the local playgrounds and touched his first basketball when he was 10. "I wanted to belong in a new neighborhood,"

Volunteers

Ernie said. "I found out fast if you wanted to belong you'd better play basketball."

So he played basketball. Only he played it better than anybody else. The kid just looking to belong became the ultimate insider: a big-time college star and an All-American.

Like Ernie Grunfeld, you may feel like an outsider. You know how it feels to be told to keep out. Your parents ask you to leave the room when they want to talk. Your sibling won't let you into his or her room. You're not sure you can get into a club at school you like.

You're not by yourself. The Hebrew people in the Bible knew about being told to keep out. Only the priests could enter God's presence and survive. Then along came Jesus to kick that barrier down and let you talk to God yourself. You do it through prayer.

Christianity is a club that doesn't let anybody in except believers in Jesus. The really cool thing is that no one who wants to join will be kept out. All it takes to get in is faith.

Write a note inviting a friend at school to your church; give it to him/her.

ANGRY BIRDS

Read James 1:19-20.

*A person's anger doesn't produce
the kind of life God wants.*

What Kevin Burnett's mother did shocked him into getting his anger under control.

As a senior in 2004, Burnett, a linebacker, was All-SEC and was drafted into the NFL. He won the Go Vols Award for community service.

But Burnett wasn't a nice kid at one time because he had a lot of anger. It came from the death of his father in a car wreck when he was 5. He stole things, he set things on fire, and he hit people. His mother, he said, "beat the mess out of me" one time when she caught him with stolen goods.

When Kevin was 9, he argued with his mama and hit her. That did it. She told him to pack a bag and took him down to the police station. She then told the desk sergeant to lock him

Volunteers

up to "[show] him what happens when you hit your mother."

When she left, Kevin was handcuffed to a bench. She went back an hour later, and he was crying. "I never want to do this again," he said. He never did.

Did you know that getting real mad is really normal? Everybody does it, not just kids. But you have to control it, just like you control the number of sodas you drink.

Think of a time you got so angry you just went wild. What did you say and do? Probably some things you wish you hadn't. Maybe you lost a friend over it. You might have even been punished for acting that way.

God isn't too keen on your getting angry either. That's because it gets in the way of your acting the way you should, the way God wants you to.

So your own anger can make God angry. Making God mad is never a good idea.

***Stand in front of a mirror and act
like you're real mad about something.
Watch how silly it makes you look.***

STOP, THIEF!

Read Exodus 20:15; 22:1-2.

You shall not steal.

Against Alabama in 1970, the Tennessee defense was nothing but a bunch of thieves. They picked off eight Tide passes! Incredible!

Bill Battle was 28 years old and the youngest head football coach in the country in 1970. That's when he took over the Vols. His first team won ten games and beat Air Force in the Sugar Bowl. The Vols also beat Alabama 24-0.

The big reason they won so easily was all that stealing. The first thief was team captain Tim Priest. He would set a Tennessee record with three interceptions that day.

By halftime, Tennessee had three interceptions and led 7-0.

Here's something strange: Alabama didn't punt the entire last half. They didn't have to. Why? Because Tennessee kept picking the ball out of the air before they had a chance to kick. The Vols stole five passes in the last half.

Stealing is taking something that belongs to someone else without their permission. It is wrong; God said so. That's all there is to it. Unless you're talking about passes in a football or basketball game. Or stealing a base in a baseball game. That's okay.

The fact is that if you steal something, you stand a good chance of winding up in jail. That's the way man's law works today.

But God's law didn't punish thieves by putting them behind bars. Instead, they had to pay back the person they had stolen from. Sometimes they had to pay back as much as five times as much as they had taken! It's called "making restitution."

Man's law or God's law — it doesn't matter. You get into trouble when you steal. Just don't ever do it.

Ask a policeman what happens if someone steals something. Then pray, asking God to keep you from temptation.

STAR POWER

Read Luke 10:1-3, 17-20.

The Lord appointed 72 others and sent them out two by two.

Cornerback Steve Johnson said the team had no superstars. One coach said it was only the fourth-most talented Tennessee team he had coached. So they were pretty bad, right? They were the 1998 national champions.

UT turned out some real superstars in the 1990s, players like Heisman-Trophy runners-up Peyton Manning and Heath Shuler. None of the many stars were around on the night of Jan. 4, 1999. That's when the Vols met Florida State in the Fiesta Bowl for the national championship. The experts saw UT didn't have any stars and picked FSU and its stars to win.

So how did this team without any stars get to this game? As that same coach put it, "It's the best team." A bunch of no-namers had

Volunteers

come together as no UT team had done since 1951. "Not one of them cares who gets the credit," said the team's strength coach.

They were no-names no more after they beat FSU 23-16 to win the national title.

Football teams and other groups may have a star. They wouldn't be much of anything, though, without everybody else to help out. How far can a star running back go without his line up front to block for him?

It's the same way with the team known as the church. Your church has a star: the pastor or preacher, who is a trained pro, the leader, the one up front of everyone on Sunday.

But Jesus didn't have any stars to help him. He just had a bunch of no-names who loved him. Nothing has changed. The church has its star. What it needs is people who aren't stars, people who do whatever they can for the sake of God's kingdom because they love Jesus.

God's church needs you.

What's your pastor's name? If he's the star, name some folks in your church who aren't stars. Tell what they do.

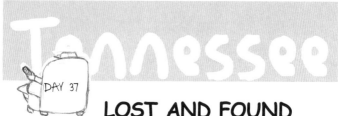

LOST AND FOUND

Read Luke 15:11-24.

The father said, "My son was lost, and now he's found."

Two UT basketball players once went looking for some late-night munches and lost a train.

In 1953, the Vols took a train to Gainesville to play Florida. The team had a one-hour wait in Atlanta. During the wait, All-Americans Ed Weiner and Carl Widseth went looking for an all-night bakery they had heard about.

"It was near midnight so we pooled our money, got a cab and made a quick trip," Weiner said. The cab driver took them to the bakery where they loaded up on cake and cookies. They climbed back into the cab with plenty of time before the train left the station.

But when they pulled into the train yard, the train was nowhere in sight. They just stood there, wondering if they had been left behind.

A train worker asked them what they were doing standing in the yard in the middle of the night. When they told him, he just laughed. Some cars had been hooked to another train, he said. He told them where they were, and the two Vols took off running.

Everybody loses things though maybe not a train. Why is it that when you lose something, it's always in the last place you look?

Have you ever heard the preacher talk about people being lost? He's not saying they need help from their GPS to find their way home from church.

When Christians talk about someone who is lost, they are speaking of people who don't know Jesus; they aren't saved. They are lost because they haven't found the only way to Heaven — through faith in Jesus.

God never leaves the lost; they leave him. And Jesus is always ready with open arms to welcome the lost people home.

Since you were born, Jesus has been looking for you. Has he found you? Do you know someone who's lost?

A BIG SUCCESS

Read Galatians 5:22, 25.

The fruit of the spirit is love, joy, peace, forbearance, kindness, goodness, faithfulness. Let us keep in step with the spirit.

A long time ago, a Tennessee football season was successful if the Vols beat Vanderbilt!

Nowadays, UT beats Vanderbilt all the time. At one point, they beat the Commodores 22 times in a row. But back in 1926, UT hired a new coach, Cpt. Bob Neyland, who was told he had one goal: Beat Vanderbilt.

At the time, UT had beaten Vandy only twice in 21 games. They had lost five straight, one of those by a score of 51-7.

It took Neyland three seasons to turn things around, but he did it. In 1928, the Vols were 7-0 when they boarded the train for Nashville. East Tennessee was going crazy for the Vols. Several trainloads of fans made the trip.

UT great Gene McEver set up a touchdown with a punt return. On fourth down, end Paul Hug caught a pass and fell across the goal line as he was tackled. After that, the Tennessee defense took over. The final score was 6-0.

Neyland wound up beating Vandy 16 times and losing only three. He was successful.

In your mind, what makes you successful? Good grades? A win by your school on the football or soccer field? New cool clothes?

How you see success will change as you get older. One day, you may think you're successful if you have a good job with a nice home and a car of your own. The world measures success that way: by how many things you have.

But all those things will pass away. The best way to measure success is spiritually. You're successful if you know Jesus Christ as your Savior. Nothing else is as important.

That kind of success makes you a true champion. And it lasts forever.

Read the Bible verse at the beginning again. How does God define success?

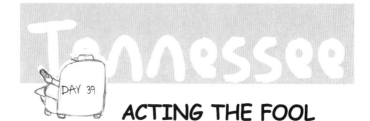

ACTING THE FOOL

Read 1 Corinthians 1:18-21.

The message of the cross seems foolish to those who do not know Jesus.

The folks in charge of athletics at UT once made a totally foolish decision: They voted to do away with football.

The 1893 season was the football program's third. It was not a good year. The Orange and White lost three games in four days by a total score of 194-0.

After that disaster, the athletic association decided to ban football in favor of baseball. After all, baseball was the school's leading sport at the time.

But a student decided to fight for football. He got a group of students to speak up in favor of football's return. He even put together a team of students that played three games.

They were all wins.

That made the athletic board take a second look at its foolish decision. It changed its mind, and Tennessee fielded a football team in 1896.

Since that foolishness, only during three wars — the Spanish-American War and the two world wars — has the University of Tennessee failed to field a football team.

You've probably acted the fool in class sometimes, haven't you? Or at home. Or with a bunch of your friends. It's fun to act the clown and make people laugh.

The Bible rightfully says that many people see the most serious thing in the history of the world — Jesus' life and death — as silly and foolish. But those people are foolish to think they're so wise that they don't need God or Jesus. They'll find out the truth one day when they meet God face to face.

Following Jesus is wise; ignoring Jesus is foolish.

***See if you can make someone laugh
by totally acting the fool.***

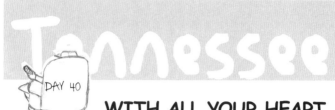

WITH ALL YOUR HEART

Read Deuteronomy 6:4-9.

Love God with all your heart, with all your soul, with all your strength.

Why would an Italian kid from New Orleans play football for Tennessee? He couldn't even understand East Tennessee English, and his dad wasn't sure about it. It was love.

In 1947, Hank Lauricella was invited to visit Ole Miss and Tennessee on a recruiting trip. Fortunately for Volunteer football history, the visit to Knoxville came first.

At once, Lauricella noticed how funny everyone talked. But he soon figured out what they were saying. He loved everything about the place. "I really enjoyed myself and decided not to bother" with Ole Miss, he said. He called the Rebels and cancelled.

When his father said LSU or Tulane would be better, the son said he had fallen in love with UT. That was good enough for dad.

As a tailback, Lauricella led UT to a 28-4-1 record his three seasons. The 1951 team won the national title. He was an All-American in 1951 and finished second in the Heisman voting. He is in the college Hall of Fame.

And he never stopped loving Tennessee.

You are a true UT fan. That means you love the Volunteers whether they win or lose. You never quit cheering for them.

That's the way you should love God. A long time ago, he told us to love him with all our heart, all our soul, and all our strength. That hasn't changed.

God wants you to love him as hard as you can. All the time. Never stop.

No matter how hard you try, you can never love God more than he loves you. You see, God loves you — with all his heart, all his soul, and all his strength.

Make a list of everybody and everything you love the most, even your pets. Just be sure God is on the list.

DAY 41

GIVING UP

Read Numbers 13:25-28, 30-32.

Some men said, "We can't attack those people because they are bigger and stronger than we are."

Susan Thornton had to lug 400 lbs. of stuff around in a little red wagon. People laughed at her and told her, "You'll never be cute doing that." But she never quit.

Thornton was UT's first great female shot putter. In high school, she was waiting around for volleyball practice to begin one day when she learned the school had a shot put. "No one knew we had one and no one knew how to use it," she said.

So she taught herself, using two socks to outline a circle and throwing into a sand pit. She also watched some shot putters on TV.

She came to Knoxville in 1976. UT didn't offer much money for women in those days, so she had to buy her own gear. And it weighed about 400 lbs. Every day, she had to carry around jump ropes, shot puts, a discus, shoes, and some medicine balls. She bought a little red wagon that she pulled all over campus.

Susan Thornton just wouldn't quit.

Most folks feels like quitting at some time or another. Maybe that sport at school is harder than you thought it was. Maybe you just can't figure out math no matter how much you study. Maybe you and a friend just don't get along anymore.

Quitting is easy. But when it comes to God, remember the story of the people of Israel. They quit when the Promised Land was theirs for the taking. They forgot that God would never, ever give up on them.

God never quits on you either. So you must never give up on God even if it seems like your prayers aren't getting through. You just don't know what God may be up to. The only way to find out is to never quit on God.

Winners never quit; quitters never win.
How does this apply to God and you?

COMEBACK KIDS

Read Acts 9:18-22.

Those who heard Paul asked, "Isn't he the one who persecuted and killed Christians in Jerusalem?"

Most folks hadn't sat down long enough to warm up their seats, and the game was over. Then the Vols pulled off a comeback

In Nov. 1991, the Vols played Notre Dame in South Bend, Ind. The Irish jumped all over UT, leading 21-0 in the first quarter! Head Vol Johnny Majors said he wondered if Notre Dame "was going to score 80 or 85" points.

In the second quarter, the Irish led 31-7. But the Vols blocked a field goal that was returned 76 yards for a score. At halftime, an excited Coach Majors jumped up on a table and shouted, "We're back in this thing."

They were. In the last half, quarterback Andy Kelly filled the air with footballs, and the defense held Notre Dame to a field goal. With nine minutes left, UT trailed only 34-28.

Kelly completed the comeback with a touchdown toss to tailback Aaron Hayden. When ND missed a field goal, UT had a 35-34 win with a comeback no one would ever forget.

A comeback means you come from behind. You know by now that you don't always win. You make an A on a test one day and sprain your ankle the next. You do all your chores at home but get in trouble for talking in class.

In life, even for a kid, winning isn't about never losing. Things will go wrong for you sometimes. Winning means you pick yourself up from your defeat and keep going. You make a comeback of your own, just the way Paul and the Volunteers did.

Besides, God's grace is always there for you, so your comeback can always be bigger than your setback. With Jesus in your life, it's not how you start that counts; it's how you finish.

Remember a time a team you like made a comeback. Compare that to a time you came back after something went wrong.

IT'S A MYSTERY

Read Romans 11:33-36.

Who has known the mind of the Lord?

Some things in football are a mystery. Like how a wide-open player can just fall down short of the goal line for no reason. It happened in a Volunteer game.

Against Alabama in 1996, Tennessee fans had trouble finding anything to cheer about. In the second quarter, Peyton Manning was sacked and fumbled at the 6-yard line. A Tide player picked up the ball and could have walked untouched into the end zone. Instead, of all things, he stumbled and fell at the 3.

The UT defense held and blocked a field-goal try. It didn't seem to matter since Bama led 13-0 in the third quarter. But the Vols rallied. Manning threw a 54-yard bomb for a touchdown. The defense got an interception for a touchdown to tie the game at 13.

Then with only 2:17 left, Jay Graham turned Neyland Stadium upside down. He ripped off a 79-yard touchdown run. UT won 20-13, a score that wouldn't have happened except for that stumble and fall nobody could explain.

Have you noticed that some things in life are just a mystery? We like to come up with answers – like questions on a quiz – but sometimes there just isn't an answer.

Do plants feel pain? How do geese know to fly in formation?

Much about God is a mystery, too. He's shown us a whole lot about himself in Jesus Christ. But not nearly everything. Like what does he really look like? How come he likes bugs so much? Where'd he get the idea for chocolate from? What does God eat?

You'll just have to wait. If you trust in Jesus, one day you and God can have a long chat. On that day, all mysteries will be cleared up.

List five things about life that are a mystery to you. Ask a parent what he/she thinks the answers are.

THAT'S CRAZY!

Read Luke 13:31–33.

Jesus said, "I must press on today and tomorrow and the next day."

UT legend Jack Reynolds had a great nickname for a linebacker: Hacksaw. His teammates called him something else: Crazy Jack.

The nicknames probably came from what Reynolds did after a loss to Ole Miss in 1969. He sawed a vehicle in half with a hacksaw! It took a dozen blades.

"Reynolds was a funny duck," said one of his coaches. One teammate recalled that when Crazy Jack was a freshman, he would sprint all-out during warmups. "It happened every day," said All-American center Bob Johnson. "Jack would run like a wild man for 17 or 18 of those 50-yard warmups. Then he'd stop and throw up his lunch."

A lot of Hacksaw's craziness was on purpose.

Volunteers

He often wore an old T-shirt that said, "Too old, too short, too slow." But that was to keep people wondering what he would do next.

What he could do was play football really well. He was All-America in 1969 and had a 14-year pro career with two Super Bowl wins.

People do some crazy things. But whether something's crazy or not depends on who is doing it. It's crazy for a teacher to want to go out for the football or softball team at school. But it's not crazy for you to do it.

It seemed crazy for Jesus to ignore warnings and go on to Jerusalem. After all, a whole bunch of people who wanted to kill him were waiting there for him.

But Jesus went because he knew he had to do what God had sent him to this Earth to do. When he did it, he would defeat our greatest enemy of all: death.

It was pretty smart after all. It meant you can be saved and have eternal life.

What's the craziest thing you've ever done? Would you do it again? Why or why not?

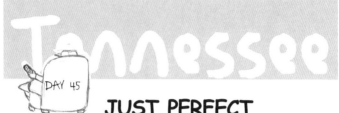

JUST PERFECT

Read Matthew 5:43-48.

Jesus said, "Be perfect, just as God is perfect."

Tennessee's defense in 1939 was just perfect. During the regular season, it didn't allow a single point!

The wins in 1939 were part of a streak of 33 straight regular-season wins for the Vols. They beat Alabama 24-0 that season. A Tide player said the Vols "ran up and down the field on us like window shades."

At one point during the long win streak, the defense shut out 17 straight teams! It went 71 quarters without a point being scored! These are two records that will never ever be broken.

The coach for all that perfection was UT legend Bob Neyland. It was said he believed in gang-tackling and the bloody nose. He was also the greatest defensive mind of his time.

Volunteers

He coached 216 games in Knoxville across 21 seasons. In 106 of those games, his defense pitched a shutout.

Including that perfect 1939 season.

Nobody's perfect. To be perfect means you never do anything wrong, you never make a mistake, you never do anything clumsy. Ever.

Oh, you can be perfect now and then. Like on a test. Or playing a song on an instrument. But you're not perfect all the time. Only one man was ever perfect. And that was Jesus.

But yet Jesus commands you to be perfect. Didn't we just say that was impossible? Has Jesus got it wrong?

Nope, not at all. When Jesus spoke of being perfect, he talked of loving perfectly as God does. To love perfectly is to love all others and not just those whom you like or who do nice things for you.

To love perfectly is to love everyone.

List three folks it's really hard for you to love. Then list something good about each one. Try to love them for that.

DAY 46

THE PRIZE

Read Philippians 3:10-14.

The heavenly prize is Jesus himself.

Vol John Finlayson once received one of the strangest honors of all: He was named All-America by a farming magazine.

A tight end, Finlayson was a three-year starter for UT from 1999-2001. He was mostly used as a blocker.

All four seasons in Knoxville, Finlayson was Academic All-SEC. He never did much to call attention to himself. Many of his classmates never knew they were sitting next to the Vols' starting tight end. "I kind of prefer it that way," he said. "I like just being a regular student."

Finlayson grew up on a farm near the Mississippi line. "We had hogs and cows and a few chickens," he said. "I mostly worked at the farm supply store my parents owned."

That agricultural background led to the All-

American award from *Successful Farming* magazine. Fellow tight end Neil Johnson joked, "I told him that *Field & Stream* is going to name him All-American next week."

Hey, we like awards, prizes, and honors, don't we? A trophy from your baseball or softball team. A certificate for good grades or perfect attendance. A medal for something good you did. Isn't it cool to have your picture in the paper?

We all like other people to notice when we have worked hard and have done a good job.

But you have to be real careful that you don't start worshipping your prizes and bragging about them. That means they become idols.

The greatest prize of all won't rust, fade, or collect dust. It's the only one worth winning. It's eternal life through Jesus Christ. God gives it to you free of charge just for trusting in Jesus.

Rank all the prizes you've won in order of how important they are to you. Compare each one to the prize of being a child of God for believing in Jesus.

WATER POWER

Read Acts 10:44-48.

Peter asked, "Can anyone keep these people from being baptized with water?"

Socks were floating down the hall of an Atlanta hotel. The UT basketball team had too much time on its hands.

The team stayed at the Peachtree Hotel for a 1953 game against Georgia Tech. All-American Ed Wiener awoke from a nap to find his roommate, J.D. Byington, standing on his bed. He was looking at the overhead sprinkler.

Byington asked how it worked, and Wiener explained it to him. He tried to go back to sleep but couldn't. "The next time I looked," he said, "J.D. was holding a match under the trigger. A moment later, we got wet."

Bells rang, fire trucks roared to the rescue, and the police showed up. Byington tossed his matches into the toilet but didn't flush them. When the emergency crews opened the door to the room, a pair of socks floated out into the hall.

They found the matches and hauled Byington to the police station. The Vol coach talked a judge out of jail time and a hefty fine. Byington did have to pay for the damages.

The Vols won the game that night 82-79.

Do you like to go swimming? Or take a boat ride? Man, the beach is cool with all that sand and sun and those waves. Is anything more fun and exciting than a big old water slide?

Water is fun, but it's a lot more than that. You need it to stay alive. You have to drink water every day.

Water is so important that it is even a part of your faith in Jesus. It's called baptism. A person who is baptized — including you — is marked by the water as someone who belongs to Jesus. It tells the world you are a Christian and that Jesus is your Lord.

Have you been baptized? If so, talk about what it was like. If not, is it time?

MUDSLINGING

Read Isaiah 1:16-19.

Your sins may be bright red, but they will be as white as snow.

Mud is one of the reasons the Vols play in beautiful Neyland Stadium today.

In 1919, the president of a local bank paid the balance owed on seven acres for use as an athletic field. The school trustees voted to name the field in honor of his wife and him: Shields-Watkins Field.

But rains in 1921 turned the field into one big mud puddle. All classes were cancelled for two days in March so students could get the field ready for play in the fall.

The first game was played on Sept. 24, 1921. It rained and the field's flat surface wouldn't drain. The student newspaper soon declared, "Fans are tired of seeing Tennessee's wonderful football teams play in a sea of mud."

Volunteers

Before the 1926 season, the field was sodded and molded so it would drain. The making of what would become awesome Neyland Stadium had begun — thanks to the mud.

Everybody knows God made mud puddles to jump into and splash the water everywhere. But when you play in the mud, you get dirty, downright filthy. You have to take a bath or shower to get clean.

It's like that when you sin, that is, do something God doesn't like. Like mud stains your clothes, sin stains your soul.

All Christians sin; so they all slip and fall into the spiritual mud. But they don't stay there. You take a spiritual bath by telling God you're sorry and asking him for forgiveness in Jesus' name. God answers by washing your soul white as snow.

As far as God is concerned, you're nice and clean again even when you're outside rolling around in the mud.

Take a bath or shower to wash your body clean. Then pray for forgiveness to wash your soul clean.

GOOD SPORTS

Read Titus 2:6-8.

Set an example: Do what is good.

After a football game in 1970, UT fans pulled off a great act of sportsmanship: They paid their respects to a coach who had left them for another SEC school.

Many Vol fans were surprised when Doug Dickey, only 31 years old, was named the head football coach after the 1963 season. The Vols needed something. They had not won more than six games in a season in six years.

Dickey "conducted a football revival in Big Orange Country." UT won the SEC in 1967 and '69. They beat Alabama three straight times. He had a six-year run of success.

Then Dickey surprised Vol fans again. He up and left to coach the Florida Gators after the 1969 season. Big Orange Country was pretty upset and angry about the whole deal.

Sure enough, Dickey and the Gators came to Knoxville in 1970. "Revenge was taken." Tennessee slaughtered Florida 34-7.

As Dickey slowly walked toward the locker room, thousands of classy UT fans gave him a standing ovation. They were thanking him for six great years. Surprised and with tears in his eyes, Dickey tipped his cap to them.

Good sportsmanship means more than just following the rules and not cheating. It means you treat the other players with respect. You don't play dirty. You don't say ugly things to them. You don't try to hurt them.

Believe it or not, the Bible talks about good sportsmanship. It's called the Golden Rule: You treat people the way that you want to be treated by them. You act that way all the time and not just while you're playing a game.

If you follow the Golden Rule in sports, at home, at school, and in all things, then you are living the way Jesus wants you to.

What sports do you play? How do you show good sportsmanship in them? What about off the field?

YOU PROMISED

Read 2 Peter 1:3-7.

God's promises are great and valuable.

It took a mighty comeback to keep head coach Butch Jones' promise alive.

In August of 2014, Jones promised the Knoxville Rotary Club the Vols would go to a bowl game that season. That meant they had to win at least six games.

It wasn't looking too good when the Vols played South Carolina. They were only 3-5 for the season and fell behind 42-28 with less than five minutes to play.

But they wouldn't quit. Quarterback Joshua Dobbs led the offense on a 75-yard drive. He scored from the 3, and it was 42-35 with 1:50 on the clock.

The defense forced a punt, and the offense roared downfield to score a touchdown. Tied at 42, the game went into overtime.

The Vols managed only a field goal, so a South Carolina touchdown would win it. They didn't get it. The defense forced a long field goal try that was no good. UT won 45-42.

When the Vols beat Vanderbilt on Nov. 29, they had six wins. They were on their way to a bowl game, just as Coach Jones had promised.

You should never make a promise lightly. That means that if you promise somebody something, you should keep it, even if it costs you or is a lot of trouble.

Sometimes your friends and even grown-ups don't keep their promises. God doesn't work that way. If God makes a promise, he keeps it, and in the Bible, God makes thousands of promises! Peter calls them God's "great and valuable" promises because God makes them and then keeps them.

You can count on God to keep his promises.

Recall the last promise you made. Whom did you make it to? Did you keep it? If you didn't keep it, why not?

SOUND OFF!

Read Revelation 5:11-13.

I heard thousands and thousands of angels singing.

In UT's drive to the '98 national title, crowd noise played a part in a big game.

The Vols hosted second-ranked Florida in the second game of the season. Few folks were thinking of Tennessee as a title contender. That changed after the Vols whipped Florida 20-17 in overtime.

The Neyland Stadium crowd was so noisy that it played a part in the game's outcome. The Gators had five turnovers and made some other mistakes because of the crowd noise. Jesse Palmer, the Gator quarterback, said it was true.

The noise made it hard to change plays at the line, Palmer said. Florida was often late getting plays into the game from the sideline.

Volunteers

That left little time to do anything with all the racket. In fact, Palmer said, the crowd noise made the situation almost impossible.

Senior Jeff Hall kicked a 41-yard field goal in overtime to break the 17-17 tie. The Gators then missed a kick for the tie.

Needless to say, the crowd went wild.

Even if you've never been to Neyland Stadium on game day, you're used to a lot of noise, aren't you? Your school is noisy; football, basketball, and soccer games are noisy. Car horns blow, dogs bark, televisions shout.

You live in a noisy world. It's fun, but if you let it, all that noise will drown out the gentle voice of God in your heart. That means you need some quiet time every day. You can say your prayers, talk to God, and then listen for what he may have to say to you.

Much about Heaven will be strange, but one thing will make you feel right at home. As the Bible says, it's a noisy place. That's because everybody's whooping it up for God.

Use a device to time yourself. Stay quiet and think about God for three minutes.

WISH UPON A STAR

Read Psalm 73:23-25.

Earth has nothing I desire besides you.

A mother at a UT game once made a wish that seemed impossible. She wished her son would score a touchdown.

The Vols of 1956 went 10-1, won the SEC, and finished No. 2 in the nation. One of the leaders was senior right tackle and captain John Gordy.

Gordy's mom was present for the Kentucky game that season. She was sitting with the mother of tailback Johnny Majors. She said her son had never scored a touchdown and wished he could. Mrs. Majors pointed out that tackles never score touchdowns.

At the Kentucky 7, the Vols gave the ball to Majors to run behind Gordy. But a UK player knocked the ball loose.

Volunteers

Incredibly, it hit Gordy right in the chest. He caught the ball and dragged two UK players with him into the end zone.

As unlikely as it was, Mrs. Gordy's wish had come true. Her son, the tackle, had scored a touchdown.

Everybody wishes for something. Maybe you wish you were older. Or you could drive. Maybe you wish for a certain video game. Or a new phone.

Wishing for something isn't bad; God put that desire in you. But sometimes what you want isn't good for you. You may want too many sodas or too much candy. You may want to see a movie that's rated too old for you.

There's a way to tell if what you wish for is good. Pray about it. God has wishes for you: He wishes you only the best. If God wants it for you, your wish will come true.

You must always want a deep and true relationship with God.

Make three wishes and pray about them. Then ask a parent whether they're good or bad for you.

IMPORTANT STUFF

Read Matthew 6:31–34.

Put God's kingdom first in your life.

Haskel Stanback knew what was important to him: pretty girls and warm weather. So he played his college football at Tennessee.

Stanback carried the load at tailback for the Vols in 1972 and '73. He considered only three schools: Georgia Tech, Ohio State, and UT. But he knew what was important to him in deciding where to play football.

One visit to Ga. Tech and its practically all-male student body wound that up. One trip to Columbus, Ohio, took care of Ohio State. "It was the first time I'd been on a plane," Stanback said. "When I flew out of Charlotte (N.C.), it was 60 degrees." When he landed in Columbus, it was snowing.

"I don't mind playing football in the snow," he said. "But I don't want to walk around in

Volunteers

snow as a regular thing." Ohio State was out.

So that left Tennessee with its campus full of pretty girls and its mild weather. While he was in Knoxville, Stanback met the pretty girl who was to become his wife.

A priority is what you regard as what's most important in your life. It's what really matters to you. It may not be pretty girls and warm weather, but it's something.

It could be anything, from making good grades to being a cheerleader one day to getting to a new level on a video game. It may even be making your parents proud of you.

The big question is whether God is one of your priorities. The truth is he should be first. God said we are to seek him first. Not second or third but first.

In Jesus, God showed you the way you are to do everything. You serve and obey him.

God — and God alone — is No. 1.

Write down ten things that are important to you. Where is God on that list? Talk about how important God is to you.

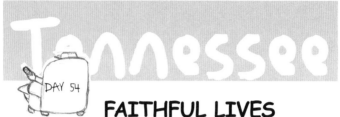

FAITHFUL LIVES

Read Hebrews 11:1-3, 6.

Without faith, you can't please God.

When UT's chances for a win seemed hopeless, cornerback Jason Allen kept the faith.

"I never thought we'd lose this game," he said. "This game" was the five-overtime 51-43 win over Alabama in 2003.

The Vol faithful must have had some doubts when Bama led 20-13 with only 1:52 left to play. But Casey Clausen led the team on an 86-yard touchdown drive that sent the game into overtime. Then the teams couldn't stop scoring, and the overtimes kept coming.

Surely the faith must have wavered when the Tide scored in the second overtime. The Vols then faced fourth and 19. No way they could pull it out. But Clausen came through with a 29-yard completion that set up a touchdown. 34-34. Third overtime.

Volunteers

40-40. Fourth OT. 43-43. Fifth OT.

Clausen ran for a 4-yard score and hit James Banks for the two-pointer. 51-43. On fourth down, Jason Allen, he of the great faith, batted a Tide pass away to end the game.

In your life, you have faith in many things. Faith in people like your parents, your grandparents, and your teachers. Faith that the Vols will win, that the family car will start, that doing the right thing is the way to live.

This is all great stuff. It makes you a great kid whom everybody likes. Someone people can count on. It makes life fun.

But nothing is as important in your life as what you believe about Jesus. To have faith in Jesus is to believe that he is the Son of God. It is to believe in his words of hope and salvation that are written in the Bible.

True faith in Jesus means more than just believing. You live for Jesus. You do everything for Jesus.

Come up with three things you can do tomorrow that will show others your faith in Jesus. Do them.

BRAG ABOUT IT

Read Job 38:8-12.

Have you ever commanded the morning to come?

Tennessee's golf coach figured that the high-school senior was just bragging. She wasn't.

Nicole Smith battled injuries as a UT golfer that ended with the 2008-09 season. She still had an outstanding college career.

In high school, she was known for her blasts from the tee. "I hit it and walk off," she said. But Smith didn't just hit the ball. One reporter said, "She wallops it about 280 to 285 yards on average."

On a recruiting trip, Smith told the Tennessee coaches what they could expect from her. She said she could really hit the ball hard. Real hard. "I don't think they believed me," she said.

Tennessee golf coach Judy Pavon sure didn't.

Volunteers

She figured she had a bragging high-schooler on her hands trying to make an impression. Smith "was saying how far she could hit it. We were saying, 'Yeah, whatever,'" Pavon said.

So Smith showed them. She stepped up to a tee and blasted away. It turned out she wasn't bragging; she was simply stating a fact.

Grown-ups like to brag about what they've done. Like putting up buildings, running for office, and buying new houses and cars. You may brag, too, about your grades, your video games, or the soccer goals you've scored.

But it all makes God laugh. We are nothing compared to God. We brag about space flight; God hung the moon, the planets, and the stars in the heavens he created. A TV weatherman guesses at the weather; God commands it. You work hard to learn math and science; God takes care of the whole universe.

You and everyone else do have one thing worth bragging about for sure: God loves you.

List three things God can brag about.
Brag to somebody that God loves you.

WHAT YOU WEAR

Read Genesis 37:1-5.

His father made Joseph a pretty coat, and his brothers hated him.

UT didn't have much money in the early days of football. So the uniforms — well, they were kind of a mess.

Get this: In 1899, some students bought a newspaper ad asking for donations to keep football alive at UT. In 1890, the expenses for a game were $10 to advertise, a dollar to mark off the field, and 40 cents for buckets, a dipper, and chewing gum. The school lost $42.35 on the game.

There just wasn't much money to spend on uniforms for the team. The players did wear jerseys, but they didn't match. They also wore stockings, but they were whatever the players could find. They were different colors.

If a player had $1.25, he could buy himself

some padded pants. They featured shields at the shins and elbows.

What pieces of uniforms there were went to the starters. The reserves had to furnish whatever they could afford.

The truth is they just didn't look too good.

You dress a certain way for school and for church. How silly would it be to wear shoes and a coat into a swimming pool?

Your clothes wear out and you outgrow them. So you change clothes all the time. Getting a new pair of shoes or some new jeans changes the way you look. It doesn't change you, does it? You're still the same person.

Do you think Jesus cares about the clothes you wear? What he cares about is your heart. What he cares about is how you act. It doesn't matter whether you're wearing clothes fit for a king or rags a homeless person might wear.

Clothes don't make you the person you are. Loving Jesus does.

Dress up in a wild outfit. In front of a mirror, act out what Jesus would say to you if he saw you.

HAVE YOU HEARD?

Mark 1:21-28.

News about Jesus spread quickly.

Tennessee's coaches once needed a kicker so badly they advertised for one! It paid off big time.

In 1975, Craig Colquitt was working in the china department of a downtown Knoxville store. One day he spotted an ad in a local news-paper. The Tennessee kicker was a senior, and the team was holding tryouts. He went. When the '75 season started, he was the team's punter.

Colquitt's first kick was a disaster. The snap from center bounced off his chest and hit his face mask. He was tackled for a safety.

Things got better after that. Craig Colquitt set a record by averaging 42.5 yards per punt for his career. He was All-SEC in 1976 and '77 and went on to kick in two Super Bowls.

Volunteers

After that, Craig's family took over. Jimmy, his nephew, broke his punting records. Then Craig's son, Dustin, kicked from 2001-05. Dustin's brother, Britton, kicked from 2006-08. They all broke Craig's records. The top four punters in UT history are all named Colquitt.

And they all came from that one ad.

Man, commercials are everywhere, aren't they? You can't escape them. Chances are your shirt has a company logo on it. That means you're a commercial with feet!

Jesus was pretty good at advertising also. He just didn't have TV or the Internet. All he had was word of mouth. All he could do was talk to people, and that's what he did. Jesus went from town to town preaching, teaching, and talking to people.

Almost two thousand years later, nothing has really changed. Talking to someone else about Jesus is still the best way to get the word out about the savior of the world.

When was the last time you told someone about Jesus? It's time to do it again.

MOVIE TIME

Read Luke 24:1-8.

Jesus is not here! He has risen!

The movie folks wouldn't make a flick out of Rick Clausen's story. It's too hokey to be real, they'd say. But it is.

Clausen started out at LSU. But the coaches told him he wasn't good enough to play quarterback in the SEC. So he transferred to Tennessee in 2002.

Clausen hoped to start against LSU in 2005. But coach Phillip Fulmer told him he wasn't good enough. So he sat on the bench while LSU led 21-0 at halftime. Fulmer put him in.

What happened was "one of the greatest comebacks in UT football history." Clausen threw a touchdown pass, but the Vols still trailed 24-7 in the fourth quarter. He led an amazing 17-point Volunteer rally that included his touchdown on a 1-yard sneak.

In overtime, Clausen got his revenge. He hit Gerald Riggs with a pass down to the 15, and Riggs scored from there. 30-27 Vols.

The quarterback LSU didn't want was 21-for-32 passing for 196 yards and two TDs. And the win. Even Hollywood wouldn't believe it.

Movies are fun, aren't they? Sitting in the dark with your family or friends watching all the action on a big screen. Chomping on some popcorn or chewing on Milk Duds.

Movies often have happy endings like Rick Clausen vs. LSU. Lots of folks will tell you that happy endings are just for the movies. Or fairy tales. That life always winds up with sadness. But that's another of the world's lies.

Jesus has been coming up with happy endings for two thousand years. When you trust in Jesus, your life will have a happy ending. One too good even for Hollywood.

With faith in Jesus, you live with God and Jesus in peace, joy, and love. Forever. The End.

List your five favorite movies.
Tell why you like them.
Do they have happy endings?

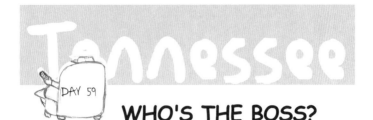

DAY 59

WHO'S THE BOSS?

Read Psalm 95:1-7.

Let us bow down and kneel in worship before our God.

Scotty Hopson did what his coach told him to. As a result, Tennessee got a last-minute basketball win over Florida.

On Jan. 31, 2010, the 15-4 Vols hosted the 15-5 Gators. Florida controlled the rebounds and led by six at halftime. The Vols fought back and took their first lead of the game at the 12:17 mark. The two teams then battled even the rest of the way. In the final minute, the Gators hit a three to lead by one.

With 24.6 seconds left, Coach Bruce Pearl called a timeout and told Hopson what to do. The coach looked at his sophomore guard and said, "Win this for us." Hopson answered, "Yes, sir." Then he went out and did it.

Hopson got the ball and dribbled some to

run down the clock. "I shot it and that's the last look I had," Hopson said. He meant he couldn't see whether the shot went in or not because a Gator had a hand in his face. But Hopson heard the home crowd roar, and he knew his shot was good.

He rebounded Florida's last shot and dribbled out the clock. He had done what his coach had told him to, and UT had a 61-60 win.

Let's face it. As a kid, just about everybody is your boss. Your parents, your teacher, your babysitter, your coaches, even older brothers and sisters. You have to do what they tell you to. You have to be obedient. If you aren't, you are in line for some serious punishment.

It's the same way with God. Like a big boss, he demands obedience from you. He wants you to live the way he tells you to in the Bible. If you're disobedient to God, what happens is that your life gets into one great big mess.

It isn't easy being obedient, even to God. But the blessings he gives you are worth it.

Think of three times you didn't do what you were told to. What happened?

HEAD GAMES

Read Job 28:20-28.

*Respect God, which will show that
you are wise.*

Tennessee football coach Bob Neyland was a master at playing head games.

Against Boston College in 1946, the Vols trailed 13-7 as the first half ended. They were hot, sweaty, and tired. But Neyland knew that Boston College was, too. So he told assistant coach Murray Warmath "to yell and run toward the dressing room."

"Our players went storming for the tunnel," Warmath said. They ran right past those tired and sweaty Boston College players. "You should have ween the [looks] on their faces," Warmath said. Tennessee blew the psyched-out BC Eagles away 33-13.

Neyland used head games on his own guys, too. In the '51 Cotton Bowl, a player missed the game-tying extra point Neyland sat down by him and put an arm around him. He said real loud, "Don't worry, son. We didn't come down here to tie." Sure enough, UT won 20-14.

Being smart is one of God's gifts. No matter what's going on, you can always use your brain to be smart and make good decisions.

Have you noticed that you use your brain all the time every day? In every class at school, you have to use your brain so you'll be smarter.

The same thing applies to your faith in God and Jesus. When you go to church or open your Bible, you keep thinking. You seek Jesus with everything you have: with your heart, your soul, your body, and your mind.

There's nothing strange about using your brain to think about God. That's because God gave you your brain to begin with. That means he likes people to be smart.

So for God, loving him and trusting in Jesus is the smartest thing of all.

Open your Bible at random and read a few verses. Use your brain to figure out what they mean as best you can.

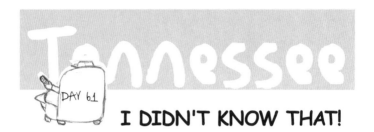

I DIDN'T KNOW THAT!

Read John 8:31-34.

You will know the truth, and the truth will set you free.

Tennessee's new women's basketball coach had a problem: She didn't know anything about the game.

Margaret Hutson was 32 when she took over the Lady Volunteers program in 1970. "She was a virtual stranger" to basketball.

So she was pretty nervous when she met with her team, sixty walk-ons. She managed to get through it with her secret. After the meeting, though, a player asked her if they were going to play pattern or freelance.

She had no idea what the girl was talking about. So she bluffed and told her it would depend upon the type of players they had. The player nodded and left.

Hutson set out to learn the game. She read

Volunteers

a bunch of books, attended some camps, and asked a men's assistant coach lots of questions. One of the counselors at a camp was a player named Pat Head, who succeeded her as UT's head coach.

Hutson learned enough to win 60 games in her four seasons as the program's boss.

When you don't know something, it's called ignorance. It doesn't mean you're a dumb bunny; you just don't know it.

That's why you go to school. To learn things. There's a whole lot you don't know. Like how they get toothpaste into the tube. How they make paper from trees. How birds can sing.

You get along all right without knowing all that stuff, don't you? But it makes a big difference if you don't know about Jesus. In that case, ignorance sets you apart from God. So you read this book and you read the Bible and you go to Sunday school to help you learn about God and Jesus.

And that's worth knowing about!

Explain how not knowing Jesus
is really a bad thing for people.

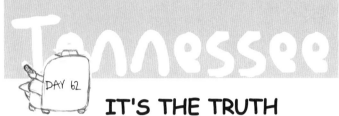

IT'S THE TRUTH

Read Matthew 5:33-37.

Jesus said, "If you mean 'yes,' say 'yes.' If you mean 'no,' say 'no.'"

Alabama's Bear Bryant and Tennessee's Bill Battle told the truth. So UT wound up with one of its most famous football players ever.

Quarterback Condredge Holloway led the Volunteers in total offense for three straight seasons (1972-74). He is a member of eight halls of fame.

He was from Huntsville, Alabama, so Alabama seemed like the place he would play. But when he asked the Bear about playing quarterback, the legend answered with the truth. "No," he said, "We're not ready for this." "This" was a black quarterback.

"What Coach Bryant did was big in my book," Holloway said. He knew Bryant could have lied and put him at defensive back.

Volunteers

When Holloway asked UT's head man the same question, Battle also told the truth. He told Holloway "if I was good enough, I could play quarterback."

That clinched it. As it turned out, Holloway was certainly good enough. He became the SEC's first black quarterback.

Have you ever told a tall tale to get out of something? Maybe your computer deleted that homework you didn't really do. Or you just forgot to clean up your room.

Sometimes we lie to get out of trouble, especially with parents. Or to make ourselves look better, or to get something we want.

But Jesus says you are always to tell the truth. As far as Jesus is concerned, telling the truth is right; lying is wrong.

Lying is what the devil ("the evil one") does. God cannot lie; the devil lies as a way of life. Whose side are you on when you tell a lie?

Recall a lie you told to get out of trouble. Did it make you feel good? Do you think God was proud of you?

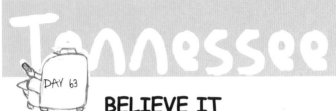

Tennessee

DAY 63

BELIEVE IT

Read John 3:16-18.

Whoever believes in Jesus will have eternal life.

Not too many people believed the Vols could whip Miami. The players did, though, and that was good enough.

On Jan. 1, 1986, Tennessee met Miami in the Sugar Bowl. The Hurricanes were ranked second in the nation; the Vols had a loss and two ties on their record. Miami had a future Heisman-Trophy winner at quarterback. The Vols had only their second-stringer.

The experts said the game "appeared to be a colossal mismatch." In other words, UT was going to get blown out of the stadium.

That their team was going to be massacred didn't keep the Orange Nation away. The fans still believed, and they showed up in droves.

So did their team. If you didn't see it, you

couldn't believe it. Tennessee played a near-perfect game and slaughtered Miami 35-7.

Miami scored first to lead 7-0. After that, it was all the Vols. They led 14-7 at halftime. In the last half, fullback Sam Henderson scored, track man Jeff Powell raced 60 yards for a TD, and Charles Wilson had a 6-yard run for a TD.

Everybody believed in the Vols now.

You believe a bunch of things without thinking about them much. That the sun will come up tomorrow. That you will have a bed to sleep in tonight. That your parents love you. And you believe Jesus is the Son of God.

But not everybody believes that part about Jesus. In fact, a lot of people, including some in your school, may well try to talk you out of believing in Jesus.

But they are really, really wrong. You just go right ahead and tell them about Jesus like he told you to. And then, say a prayer for them that they will come to believe as you do.

***Make a list of some things you believe.
What if you didn't believe them?
How would your life be different?***

DAY 64

THE PROPHET

Read Isaiah 53:6-9.

He went like a lamb to the
slaughter and said not a word.

Nancy Lay saw the future of women's college sports and didn't want to be a coach in it. So she stepped aside.

Lay pretty much began women's athletics at Tennessee. A graduate student in 1960, she re-established the women's basketball program. Until 1968, she coached women's basketball, volleyball, and tennis.

Her players were mostly PE majors. Anyone could try out for volleyball just by signing up. Volleyball players piled into cars for road trips and paid for the gas themselves. They stayed in dorms. One time Lay handed out toenail clippers to the winner of a tournament. "They were like a hundred for a dollar," she said.

But in the late 1960s, Lay became something

of a prophet. She correctly saw women's basketball becoming big-time athletics in the near future. "I knew what was coming," she said. She was a teacher first and didn't want to be a full-time coach. So she resigned.

She did, however, have a hand in shaping the future by helping to hire Pat Head Summitt as the women's basketball coach.

In the Old Testament, you read a lot about God's prophets. Isaiah was one. Did those guys walk around predicting the future like some scary palm reader? Not really.

Instead, they delivered a word that God had given them. Sometimes — as when Isaiah spoke of Jesus' suffering and death — that involved the future. But typically, the prophets told the people what God wanted them to do, how God said they should live.

Where is your prophet? How can you find out what God wants you to do? You read the Bible and you pray. It's all right there for you.

Write down five predictions (like your next test grade). Check them later to see how many you got right.

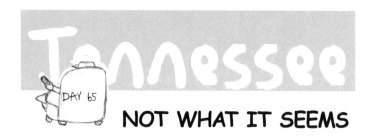

NOT WHAT IT SEEMS

Read Habakkuk 1:2-4.

*God, why do you put up with the
wrong things people are doing?*

When Ron Slay played, things on the basketball court weren't always what they seemed.

Slay was once called "a bona fide flake." He
showed up for his first Volunteer practice in
1999 wearing a mask like those in the horror
movie *Scream*. It was said he talked and
clowned around all the time on the court.

But Slay was a very good player. As a senior
in 2002-03, he was the SEC Player of the Year.

In the opening round of the 2000 NCAA
Tournament, Slay's all-out play and his zany
antics had the other team shook up. "They
looked at me like I wanted to bite 'em or
something," he said.

With 13.3 seconds left, he scored to give UT
a 60-58 lead. He was bumped and crashed to

the floor, rolling around in pain. The refs said it was a brutal assault and called it a flagrant foul. That meant UT got two free throws and the ball. Tennessee won 63-58.

When the game ended, Slay had apparently had some miraculous healing from his awful injury. He bounced around in celebration. It seems he had faked his injury.

You know, sometimes things just aren't what they seem. It's like a mirror in a fun house at the fair. Have you ever seen one of those? It makes you look all wacky and distorted.

It's that way with the world; it looks like nobody's in charge. We have wars everywhere. People hurt and kill other people. Children go to bed hungry at night. What's going on?

That's what Habakkuk asked God long ago, and God answered him. God said things aren't what they seem. He said he was in control and one day he would make everything all right.

We just have to trust and believe in God.

As Habakkuk did, name some things you'd like to see God change about this world. Pray for those changes.

DAY 66

NAME IT!

Read Exodus 3:13-15.

Moses asked God what his name was. God answered, "Tell them I AM has sent you."

The 1905 football season was a pretty bad one for the Orange and White except for one big thing: The team got itself a nickname.

Tennessee's football team went 3-5-1. They beat the Tennessee School for the Deaf, American University, and the Centre College Praying Colonels. Not exactly big-time football. The Vols beat American 104-0, which is still the school scoring record for a single game.

The 1905 team was the first one to play as the "Volunteers." In the spring, that nickname first appeared in local newspapers.

The nickname arose long before UT began playing football. Large numbers of Tennessee boys volunteered for the War of 1812. Then

Volunteers

during the Mexican War of 1846-48, the governor issued a call for 2,800 men. 30,000 Tennessee men answered his call.

The state became known as the "Volunteer State," and the UT nickname followed.

Your name is not just a label to keep people from hollering, "Hey, you" at you all the time. When your friends and classmates hear your name, they think of something about you.

This is really true in the Bible. The names of people in the Bible told other people something about them. Maybe how they acted. Or if they were strong or godly people.

The same is true of the name of God. At Mt. Horeb, God told Moses what his name was: Yahweh or "I Am." God told us his name as another way to let us get close to him. You have to know someone's name to be a friend.

As for you, what do you think your name says about you to God? Remember this: Just as you know God's name, he knows yours, too.

Have an adult help you look up the meaning of your first name. Does it match who you are and what you're like?

TOP SECRET

Read Romans 2:1-4, 16.

One day, God will appoint Jesus to judge everyone's secret thoughts.

The national champions of 1998 had a big secret that kept them undefeated: a stick.

The week before the Alabama game, a good friend sent head coach Phillip Fulmer, a hiker, a walking stick. It had his name and "Tennessee Vols" carved on it. Fulmer took the stick to practice "just to show the players." They got a big kick out of it, laughing that Fulmer looked like Moses with his staff.

That night Fulmer thought about it. He saw that the Moses image was a good one. He had led his people to the Promised Land. For the Vols, the Promised Land was a national title.

So he told the team the stick would help lead them to an undefeated season. It would help give them energy and remind them to

Volunteers

focus on winning the next game.

The stick was to be their secret. "Can't tell your girlfriend, your parents, no one," he said.

The players bought into it. The stick went everywhere with them the rest of the season. "One player carried it with pride and our players made it work," Fulmer said.

All the way to an undefeated season.

You probably have some secrets you keep from certain people. Do you tell your sisters and brothers everything? How about your mom and dad? Maybe there's a girl or a boy at school or at church that you really like but you haven't told anyone.

You can keep some secrets from the world. You must never think, though, that you can keep a secret from God. God knows everything: all your mistakes, all your sins, all the bad things you say or think.

But here's something that's not a secret: No matter what God knows about you, he still loves you. Enough to die for you on a cross.

Does it make you feel good or bad that God knows all your secrets? Why?

WILD AND CRAZY

Read Acts 4:13-14.

The leaders realized Peter and John were ordinary men. That surprised them.

Tennessee's win over Georgia Tech in 2017 was so wild and crazy that one writer called the Vols "team chaos."

The truth is that the Yellow Jackets just plain old kicked the stuffings out of the Vols. They ran for 535 yards, the most ever against Tennessee in its history! Tech had the ball more than twice as long as Tennessee did.

But as head coach Butch Jones said, the Vols used "character and grit" to stay close. With five minutes left, Tech led 28-21 but had only to kick a field goal to wrap the game up.

Crazily, Tech fumbled. Then the Vols, who hadn't done much with the ball all game, went 93 yards and tied it up with 1:29 left to play.

John Kelly got the touchdown.

In the second overtime, Tech went for two points to win it. It was a crazy play. If the quarterback had pitched the ball backwards, Tech would have scored and won. But the ball went forward and hit the ground. Incomplete pass.

UT won this wild and crazy game 42-41.

Some football games do get wild and crazy, don't they? Did you know that Jesus calls you to a wild and crazy life? One that is full of adventure like Peter and John had.

Chances are, though, that you think church is boring most of the time. That's because you are not being wild and crazy for Jesus.

Jesus doesn't want you to sit around. He wants you to get up and get out. Sing in a choir. Ride your bike with a Jesus tag on it. Go to Christian camps. Help old folks when you get the chance. Pray for other kids.

Being a Christian isn't supposed to be dull. It should be wild and crazy.

With an adult's help, come up with a wild and crazy thing or two you can do for Jesus. Then do them.

STORY TIME

Read Luke 8:36-39.

As Jesus had ordered him to, the man told all over town that Jesus had healed him.

Track scholarship but a Hall-of-Fame basketball player. A roommate's murder. Olympian who didn't get to play. Holly Warlick has a story to tell.

Warlick arrived on the UT campus in 1976 with a scholarship for the 400-meter run. She walked on to the basketball team as just about everybody did in those days.

She was the starting point guard for four seasons and a three-time All-America. She was called the "best player in the South." Her senior year she became the first UT player of either gender to have her jersey retired.

Warlick was picked for the 1980 Olympic team, the one the U.S. boycotted.

Volunteers

After her graduation from Tennessee, she played one season of pro ball. She broke a wrist and her nose, the paychecks stopped coming, and her roommate was murdered. She still led the team to the title.

Warlick is in five halls of fame. Prior to the 2012-13 season, she was named the Lady Vols' head coach, succeeding Pat Summitt.

Like Holly Warlick, you have a story to tell. It's the story of your life. Nobody else in the world has one like it. Part of that story is how you met Jesus. It's the most important chapter of all.

Too many people are shy about talking of Jesus to other people. It's called "witnessing." They say, "I just don't know what to say."

But witnessing is nothing but telling your story. No one can say it isn't true because it is. You just tell your friends or a member of your family the beautiful, awesome story of Jesus and you.

Tell a parent your story about how you met Jesus.

TRAGEDY

Read Job 1:13-22.

*In all this, Job did not sin by
charging God with wrongdoing.*

The most awful day in the history of Tennessee football was Oct. 18, 1965.

It was a great weekend. The Vols had played hard and had tied an Alabama team that was supposed to beat them. That left everybody feeling pretty good.

But then at 6:53 a.m. the following Monday, a passenger train slammed into a car. In it were three UT assistant coaches on their way to work. Killed on the scene were Bill Majors, the 26-year-old brother of Johnny Majors (the UT head football coach from 1977-92), and end coach Bob Jones, 30. Offensive line coach Charlie Rash, 28, died four days later.

UT had never known tragedy like that. As team captain Hal Wantland put it, "You just don't play for coaches; you learn to love them and respect them."

The Houston Cougars, the next opponent, offered to cancel the game, but the decision was made to play. The players wore black crosses on their helmets and won 17-8.

Maybe you know somebody like Job who has had terrible things happen to them. Maybe something bad has happened to you, your family, or a friend.

Bad things happen to good people like those UT coaches and their families. It's just a fact of life. It's easy to think when bad things happen that God is punishing you for some sin in your life. But that's not true. Job's story helps people understand that. The Bible says rain falls on good people and bad people.

When tragedy comes in our lives, we must do what Job did. We don't have to like it; we can even get mad with God about it. What we must never do is lose our faith in God.

Find three terrible things that happened to Job. What does it mean that the Lord gives and the Lord takes away?

NOTES

(by devotion number)

1   A man who had played . . . went to the movies.: Russ Bebb, *The Big Orange* (Huntsville, AL: The Strode Publishers, 1973), pp. 24-26.
2   to grab "a few whiffs of oxygen": Tom Mattingly, "Sines Did Sears One Better, Scheduled Doubleheader," *Knoxville News Sentinel*, Dec. 7, 2008.
3   He had never practiced . . . listed on the roster.: Graham Watson, "Tennessee Grabs Last-Second Kicker," *Dr. Saturday*, Nov. 8, 2011, http://rivals.yahoo.com/ncaa/football/blog/dr_saturday/post.
3   So they called at his . . . him to the stadium.: Wes Rucker, "Brodus, Buddies and 'Burgers," *GoVols247*, http://tennessee247sports.com/Article.
4   "a genuine beauty . . . hair and brown eyes.": Pat Summitt with Sally Jenkins, *Raise the Roof* (New York: Broadway Books, 1998), p. 86.
4   Clement showed up for . . . said with a smile.: Summitt with Jenkins, pp. 197-98.
5   "I [thought I could . . . to take the ball,": Mike Strange, "Denney Still Recalls How UT Faked Out Syracuse in '66," *Knoxville News Sentinel*, Sept. 3, 1998.
5   Denney outfought two Syracuse players: Strange, "Denney Still Recalls."
6   In 1925, Cpt. Robert . . . had begun at UT.: Marvin West, *Legends of the Tennessee Vols* (Champaign, Ill.: Sports Publishing L.L.C., 2005), pp. 1, 3.
7   Growing up, Antone Davis . . . he had done it.: Ray Glier, *What It Means to Be a Volunteer* (Chicago: Triumph Books, 2008), pp. 192-195.
8   He knew nothing about . . . had earned his respect.": Gus Manning and Haywood Harris, *Once a Vol, Always a Vol!* (Champaign, Ill.: Sports Publishing L.L.C., 2006), pp. 153-54.
8   who had a veteran . . . stand excuse-making: Manning Harris, p. 158.
9   He called his dad . . . to happen to me.": Brad Shepard, "Tennessee Football: OL Jacob Gilliam Is College Football's Ultimate Warrior," *BleacherReport.com*, Oct 29, 2014, http://www.bleacherreport.com/article/2248413/tennessee-football-ol-jacob-gilliam-is-college-footballs-ultimate-warrior.
10 To recruit Mayo, line coach . . . to do with that snake.": Marvin West, *Tales of the Tennessee Vols* (Champaign, Ill.: Sports Publishing L.L.C., 2001), pp. 106-07.
11 There were no scholarships. . . . she could get it.: Randy Moore, *Hoop Tales: Tennessee Lady Vols* (Guilford, Conn.: The Globe Pequot Press, 2005), pp. 30-35.
12 During that goal-line . . . get him off the field.": Bob Gilbert, *Neyland: The Gridiron General* (Savannah, Ga.: Golden Coast Publishing Co., 1990), pp. 184-85.
13 When he was 9, . . . from the dining hall.: West, *Legends of the Tennessee Vols*, pp. 117-19.
14 Head coach Pat Summitt called . . . sank three straight shots: Alan Ross, *Seven* (Nashville: Cumberland House, 2007) pp. 77-78.
14 After the game, Summitt . . . canal to save it.: Ross, *Seven*, p. 78.
15 George Cafego always called it a . . . tie he ever owned.: West, *Legends of the Tennessee Vols*, pp. 46, 48-49.
16 Vols head coach Johnny Majors . . . the school had ever taken.: Mike Strange, "Vols' 1980 Victory Against Auburn Came from Nowhere," *The Knoxville News Sentinel*, Oct. 1, 1998.
16 Auburn's head coach said . . . among all these Indians.": Strange, "Vols' 1980 Victory."
17 Since Wyche had seen . . . have to stand up.: Chris Cawood, *Legacy of the Swamp Rat* (Kingston, TN: Magnolia Hill Press, 1994), pp. 76, 80.
17 When the game was . . . biggest hugs ever.: Cawood, *Legacy of the Swamp Rat*, p. 80.

18   On the day before the . . . "I got you, Coach.": "Connor Shaw Hurt as No. 11 South
           Carolina Falls to Tennessee," *ESPN.com*, Oct. 19, 2013, scores. espn.go.com/ncf/
           recap?gameid=332922633.
19   Coach and I never talked about it,: Mike Strange, "Robinson a Pioneer," *The Knoxville
           News Sentinel*, Feb. 28, 2006.
19   "the perfect man for . . . accepted wholeheartedly," Strange, "Robinson a Pioneer."
20   The first game of his . . . ball away and running.: Cawood, pp. 215-16.
21   "When people are going . . . to see that stuff,": Gary Lundy, "Vols Adapt to Late-Night
           Kickoff in Different Ways," *The Knoxville News Sentinel*, Oct. 15, 2004.
22   "There was no panic," . . . to find a way.": Mike Strange, "Hail Yes," *Knoxville News*, Oct.
           1, 2016, http://www.knoxnews.com/sports/vols/football/hail-jauan-vols-beat-
           georgia-in-final-seconds-34-31.
22   "the best ball of his career": Edward Aschoff, "Stuff You Dream About," *ESPN.com*, Oct. 2,
           2016, http://www.espn.com/blog/sec/post/_/id/121664/-how-tennessee-pulled-off-
           its-miracle-win-over-georgia.
23   Tennessee had never tried . . . known as "The Stop.": Randy Moore, *Stadium Stories:
           Tennessee Volunteers* (Guilford, CN: The Globe Pequot Press, 2004), pp. 64, 66.
24   The head coach saw . . . college ball anywhere,: Glier, pp. 142-43.
24   At a coaches' meeting . . . they became good friends.: Glier, pp. 142.-43.
24   A Notre Dame lineman . . . I will see all year.: Glier, p. 143.
25   All these strange things about early college football are found in the book *War Eagle* by
           Clyde Bolton (Huntsville, AL: The Strode Publishers, 1973).
26   One time at practice, . . . to take on Kiner.": West, *Legends of the Tennessee Vols*, p. 43.
27   In 1901, the teams met . . . the score tied at six.: Bebb, p. 58.
28   The Temple coach knew . . . had something to watch.: Mike Strange, "Night Crawler,"
           Knoxville News Sentinel, Nov. 8, 2007.
29   Center Bob Davis was . . . the game's only score.: Mike Strange, "In '50 Game, Vols Put
           Freeze on Wildcats' Dreams," *Knoxville News Sentinel*, Nov. 19, 1998.
30   A long time ago women . . . ankles and little lungs.: Debby Schriver, *In the Footsteps of
           Champions* (Nashville: The University of Tennessee Press, 2008), p. xxii.
30   They could do croquet . . . tournament in 1959.: Schriver, *In the Footsteps of Champions*,
           p. xxii.
31   He was 5-10 and . . . ballooned to 330 pounds.: West, *Legends of the Tennessee Vols*,
           p. 67.
31   I can usually tell . . . to be [any good]." West, *Legends of the Tennessee Vols*, p. 70.
31   The NYU coach asked . . . didn't hear him.": West, *Legends of the Tennessee Vols*, p. 69.
31   The strangest thing . . . ate his words.: West, *Legends of the Tennessee Vols*, p. 71.
32   He was late for . . . just an old swamp rat. West, *Legends of the Tennessee Vols*, p. 111.
32   He trotted into the . . . hum that tater.": West, *Legends of the Tennessee Vols*, p. 113.
33   His family fled Romania . . . you'd better play basketball.": *Randy Moore, Hoop Tales:
           Tennessee Volunteers Men's Basketball* (Guilford, CN: The Globe Pequot Press,
           2005), p. 89.
34   It came from the death . . . want to do this again,": John Adams, "From the Mean Streets,"
           Knoxville News-Sentinel, Aug. 17, 2003.
35   Alabama didn't punt the . . . a chance to kick.: Cawood, p. 127.
36   Cornerback Steve Johnson said . . . team he had coached.: Moore, *Stadium Stories*,
           pp. 146-47.
36   "It's the best team. . . . who gets the credit,": Moore, *Stadium Stories*, pp. 146-47.
37   In 1953 the Vols took . . . Vols took off running.: West, *Tales of the Tennessee Vols*,
           p. 233.
38   back in 1926, . . . one goal: Beat Vanderbilt.: Bebb, p. 126.
38   East Tennessee was going . . . as he was tackled.: Mike Strange, "28 Vols Ended

Domination by Beating Commodores," *Knoxville News Sentinel*, Nov. 23, 2000.

39 After that disaster, the athletic . . . a football team in 1896.: Bebb, p. 29.

40 In 1947, Hank Lauricella . . . good enough for dad.: West, *Legends of the Tennessee Vols*, pp. 63, 65.

41 "You'll never be cute doing that.": Schriver, p. 24.

41 she was waiting around . . . pulled all over campus.: Schriver, pp. 23-24.

42 Johnny Majors said he . . . 80 or 85" points.: West, *Tales of the Tennessee Vols*, p. 46.

42 At halftime, an excited . . . back in this thing.": West, *Tales of the Tennessee Vols*, p. 47.

43 A Tide player picked up . . . untouched into the end zone.: Al Browning, *Third Saturday in October* (Nashville: Cumberland House, 2001), p. 362.

44 He sawed a vehicle . . . throw up his lunch.": West, *Legends of the Tennessee Vols*, p. 91.

44 He often wore an . . . he might do next.: West, *Legends of the Tennessee Vols*, p. 95.

45 the Vols "ran up and down the field on us like window shades.": William Nack, "Absolute Zero," *Sports Illustrated*, Dec. 28, 1998, http://sportsillustrated.cnn.com/vault/article/magazine/MAG1014895/index.htm.

45 he believed in gang-tackling and bloody noses.: Nack, "Absolute Zero."

46 Many of his classmates . . . All-American next week.": Mike Griffith, "Hometown Hero," *Knoxville News Sentinel*, Aug. 31, 2000.

47 The team stayed at . . . pay for the damages.: West, *Tales of the Tennessee Vols*, pp. 145-46.

48 In 1919, the president . . . play in the fall.: Barry Parker and Robin Hood, *Neyland: Life of a Stadium* (Chattanooga: Parker Hood Press, Inc., 2000), pp. 4-5.

48 "Fans are tired of . . . so it would drain.: Parker and Hood, pp. 7-8.

49 "conducted a football revival in Big Orange Country.": West, *Legends of the Tennessee Vols*, p. 121.

49 "Revenge was taken." . . . tipped his cap to them.: West, *Legends of the Tennessee Vols*, p. 126.

50 In August of 2014, . . . bowl game that season.: Dustin Dopirak, "Vols Not Shying Away from Bowl Game," *Knoxville News Sentinel*, Nov. 22, 2014, http://nl.newsbank.com/nl-search/we/Archives?p_action=doc&p_docid=151C1CEDC9FA0038.

51 The noise made it hard . . . situation almost impossible.: Gary Lundy, "Florida Felt 5 Turnovers Contributed to Its Demise," *Knoxville News Sentinel*, Sept. 20, 1998.

52 Gordy's mom was present . . . into the end zone.: West, *Tales of the Tennessee Vols*, p. 242.

53 He considered only three . . . Ohio State and UT.: Manning and Harris, p. 177.

53 "It was the first time . . . it was 60 degrees.": Mike London, "Friday Night Legends: Snapping Back with Stanback," *salisburypost.com*, Nov. 7, 2008, http://www.salisburypost.com/Sports/110708-london-s-legend.

53 "I don't mind playing . . . as a regular thing.": Manning and Harris, p. 177.

53 While he was in . . . to become his wife.: London, "Friday Night Legends."

54 "I never thought we'd lose this game,": Mike Strange, "Marathon Men," *Knoxville News Sentinel*, Oct. 26, 2003.

55 "I hit it and walk off," . . . tee and blasted away.: Dan Fleser, "Smith Likes Hitting First," *Knoxville News Sentinel*, April 14, 2006.

56 In 1899, some students bought . . . football alive at UT: Bebb, pp. 35-36.

56 In 1890, the expenses for . . . whatever they could afford.: Bebb, pp. 37-38.

57 In 1975, Craig Colquitt was . . . he was the team's punter.: Glier, p. 130.

57 Colquitt's first kick was a . . . hit his face mask.: Glier, p. 132.

58 coach Phillip Fulmer told him he wasn't good enough.: Mark Burgess, "Clausen Writes a Storybook Finish," *Knoxville News Sentinel*, Sept. 27, 2005.

58 "one of the greatest comebacks in UT football history.": "Reliving the Tennessee Volunteers 2005 Football Season," *viewfromrockytop.com*, July 20, 2008, http://www.viewfromrockytop.com/category/tennessee-volunteer-football/players-rick-clausen.

59 "Win this for us." . . . his shot was good.: Drew Edwards, "Second-Half Rebounds Prove Heroic Like Hopson," *UTSPORTS*.com, Jan. 31, 2010, http://www.utsports.com/sports/m-baskbl/spec-rel/013110aaa.html.

60 Against Boston College in . . . the [looks] on their faces,": West, *Legends of the Tennessee Vols*, p. 5.

60 In the '51 Cotton Bowl, . . . down here to tie.": Gilbert, *Neyland*, pp. 186-87.

61 "She was a virtual stranger" . . . player nodded and left.: Moore, *Hoop Tales: Tennessee Lady Volunteers*, pp. 41-42.

61 Hutson set out to . . . player named Pat Head,: Moore, *Hoop Tales: Tennessee Lady Volunteers*, p. 44.

62 when he asked the Bear . . . put him at defensive back.: Glier, p. 111.

62 When Holloway asked UT's . . . I could play quarterback.: Glier, p. 109.

63 the game "appeared to be a colossal mismatch.": Moore, *Stadium Stories*, p. 115.

64 Her players were mostly . . . They stayed in dorms.: Schriver, p. xxvi.

64 One time Lay handed . . . hundred for a dollar,": Moore, *Hoop Tales: Tennessee Lady Volunteers*, p. 18.

64 "I knew what was coming,": *Hoop Tales: Tennessee Lady Volunteers*, p. 18.

65 Slay was once called . . . time on the court.: Moore, *Hoop Tales: Tennessee Volunteers Men's Basketball*, p. 181.

65 "They looked at me . . . had faked his injury.: Moore, *Hoop Tales: Tennessee Volunteers Men's Basketball*, p. 185.

66 during the Mexican War . . . men answered the call.: Bebb, p. 70.

67 The week before the . . . players made it work.: Phillip Fulmer with Jeff Hagood, *A Perfect Season* (Nashville: Rutledge Hill Press, 1999), pp. 96-98.

68 one writer called the Vols "team chaos.": Barrett Sallee, "'Team Chaos' Is Back," CBS Sports, Sept. 5, 2017, http://www.cbssports.com/college-football/news/team-chaos-is-back-as-tennessee-once-again-finds-a-way-in-2ot-vs-georgia-tech/.

68 as head coach Butch Jones . . . "character and grit" to stay close.: Sallee, "'Team Chaos' Is Back."

68 If the quarterback had pitched . . . and hit the ground.: Andy Staples, "Tennessee Gets the Last Laugh," *SI.com*, Sept. 5, 2017, http://www.si.com/college-football/2017/09/05/tennessee-georgia-tech-overtime-win-butch-jones.

69 the "best player in the South.": "Holly Warlick," *Tennessee Circle of Influence: 2009-10 Lady Vol Basketball*, p. 27, http://www.utladyvols.com/sports/w-baskbl/spec-rel/tennw-2w-baskbl-mg2008.html.

69 She broke a wrist . . . roommate was murdered.: Mike Strange, "It's Pretty Incredible," *Knoxville News Sentinel*, June 9, 2001.

70 "You just don't play . . . offered to cancel the game,: Bebb, pp. 320, 322.

WORKS USED

Adams, John. "From the Mean Streets to Monster Hits — Cover Story: Kevin Burnett." *Knoxville News-Sentinel.* 17 Aug. 2003.

Aschoff, Edward. "'Stuff You Dream About': Inside Tennessee's Miracle Win over Georgia." *ESPN. com.* 2 Oct. 2016. http://www.espn.com/blog/sec/post/_/id/121664/how-tennessee-pulled-off-its-miracle-win-over-georgia.

Bebb, Russ. *The Big Orange: A Story of Tennessee Football.* Huntsville, AL: The Strode Publishers, 1973.

Bolton Clyde. *War Eagle: A Story of Auburn Football.* Huntsville, AL: The Strode Publishers, 1973.

Browning, Al. *Third Saturday in October: The Game-by-Game Story of the South's Most Intense Football Rivalry.* Nashville: Cumberland House, 2001.

Burgess, Mark. "Clausen Writes a Storybook Finish for UT; Backup QB Defeats Former Team-mates." *Knoxville News Sentinel.* 27 Sept. 2005.

Cawood, Chris. *Legacy of the Swamp Rat: Tennessee Quarterbacks Who Said No to Alabama.* Kingston, TN: Magnolia Hill Press, 1994.

"Connor Shaw Hurt as No. 11 South Carolina Falls to Tennessee." *ESPN.com.* 19 Oct. 2013. scores.espn.go.com/ncf/recap?gameid=332922633.

Dopirak, Dustin. "Vols Not Shying Away from Bowl Game." *Knoxville News Sentinel.* 22 Nov. 2014. http://nl.newsbank.com/nl-search/we/Archives?p_action=doc&p_docid=15C1CEDC9FA0038.

Edwards, Drew. "Second-Half Rebounds Prove Heroic Like Hopson." *UTSPORTS.com.* 31 Jan. 2010. http://www.utsports.com/sports/m-baskbl/spec-rel/013110aaa.html.

Fleser, Dan. "Smith Likes Hitting First . . . Long; Freshman Golfer Plays Key Role for Lady Vols." *Knoxville News Sentinel.* 14 April 2006.

Fulmer, Phillip with Jeff Hagood. *A Perfect Season.* Nashville: Rutledge Hill Press, 1999.

Gilbert, Bob. *Neyland: The Gridiron General.* Savannah, Ga.: Golden Coast Publishing Co., 1990.

Glier, Ray. *What It Means to Be a Volunteer: Phillip Fulmer and Tennessee's Greatest Players.* Chicago: Triumph Books, 2008.

Griffith, Mike. "Hometown Hero: Finlayson the Farmer Still Producing as UT Tight End." *Knoxville News Sentinel.* 31 Sug. 2000.

"Holly Warlick: 25th Season at Tennessee." *Tennessee Circle of Influence: 2009-10 Lady Vol Basketball.* 26-27. http://www.utladvols.com/sports/w-baskbl/spec-rel/tennw-w-baskbl-mg2008.html.

London, Mike. "Friday Night Legends: Snapping Back with Stanback." salisburypost.com. 7 Nov. 2008. http://www.salisburypost.com/Sports/110708-london-s-legend.

Lundy, Gary. "Florida Felt 5 Turnovers Contributed to Its Demise." *Knoxville News Sentinel.* 20 Sept. 1998.

-----. "Vols Adapt to Late-Night Kickoff in Different Ways." *Knoxville News Sentinel.* 15 Oct. 2004.

Manning, Gus and Haywood Harris. *Once a Vol, Always a Vol! The Proud Men of the Volunteer Nation.* Champaign, Ill.: Sports Publishing L.L.C., 2006.

Mattingly, Tom. "Sines Did Sears One Better, Scheduled Doubleheader." *Knoxville News Sentinel.* 7 Dec. 2008.

Moore, Randy. *Hoop Tales: Tennessee Lady Volunteers.* Guilford, Conn.: The Globe Pequot Press, 2005.

-----. *Hoop Tales: Tennessee Volunteers Men's Basketball.* Guilford, CN: The Globe Pequot Press, 2005.

-----. *Stadium Stories: Tennessee Volunteers: Colorful Tales of the Orange and White.* Guilford, CN: The Globe Pequot Press, 2004.

Nack, William. "Absolute Zero." *Sports Illustrated.* 28 Dec. 1998. http://sportsillustrated.cnn.com/vault/article/magazine/MAG1014895/index.htm.

"Reliving the Tennessee Volunteers 2005 Football Season: Part 4, LSU and the Rally in the Valley." *viewfromrockytop.com.* 20 July 2008. http://www.viewfromrockytop.com/

category/tennessee-volunteer-football/players//rick-clausen.

Ross, Alan. *Seven: The National Championship Teams of the Tennessee Lady Vols*. Nashville: Cumberland House, 2007.

Rucker, Wes. "Brodus, Buddies and 'Burgers." *GoVols247*. http://tennessee247sports.com/ Article.

Sallee, Barrett. "'Team Chaos Is Back as Tennessee Once Again Finds a Way in 2OT vs. Georgia Tech." *CBSSports*. 5 Sept. 2017. http://www.cbssports.com/college-football/news/ team-chaos-is-back-as-tennessee-once-again-finds-a-way-in-2ot-vs-georgia-tech/.

Schriver, Debby. *In the Footsteps of Champions: The University of Tennessee Lady Volunteers, the First Three Decades*. Nashville, TN: The University of Tennessee Press, 2008.

Shepard, Brad. "Tennessee Football: OL Jacob Gilliam Is College Football's Ultimate Warrior." *BleacherReport.com*. 29 Oct 2014. http://www.bleacherreport.com/article/2248413/ tennessee-football-ol-jacob-gilliam-is-college-footballs-ultimate-warrior.

Staples, Andy. "Tennessee Gets the Last Laugh with Tenacious Comeback Win over Georgia Tech." *SI.com*. 5 Sept. 2017. http://www.si.com/college-football/2017/09/05/tennessee-georgia-tech-overtime-win-butch-jones.

Strange, Mike. "28 Vols Ended Domination by Beating Commodores. *Knoxville News Sentinel*. 23 Nov. 2000.

-----. "Denney Still Recalls How UT Faked Out Syracuse in '66." *Knoxville News Sentinel*. 3 Sept. 1998.

-----. "Hail Yes: Vols Beat Georgia in Final Seconds, 34-31." *Knoxville News*. 1 Oct. 2016. http:// www.knoxvillenews.com/sports/vols/football/hail-jauan-vols-beat-goergia-in-final-seconds.

-----. "In '50 Game, Vols Put Freeze on Wildcats' Dream of Title." *Knoxville News Sentinel*. 19 Nov. 1998.

-----. "It's Pretty Incredible: Warlick at Home in Hall." *Knoxville News Sentinel*. 9 June 2001.

-----. "Marathon Men: Clausen Leads UT Past Alabama in Five OTs." *Knoxville News Sentinel*. 26 Oct. 2003.

-----. "Night Crawler: Temple Set Stage in Knoxville for Time Clock." *Knoxville News Sentinel*. 8 Nov. 2007.

-----. "Robinson a Pioneer: First UT Black on Court of Orange and White." *Knoxville News Sentinel*. 28 Feb. 2006.

-----. "Vols' 1980 Victory Against Auburn Came from Nowhere." *Knoxville News Sentinel*. 1 Oct. 1998.

Summitt, Pat with Sally Jenkins. *Raise the Roof: The Inspiring Inside Story of the Tennessee Lady Vols' Undefeated 1997-98 Season*. New York: Broadway Books, 1998.

Watson, Graham. "Tennessee Grabs Last-Second Kicker off His Frat House Couch." *Dr. Saturday*. 8 Nov. 2011. http://rivals.yahoo.com/ncaa/football/blog/dr_saturday/post.

West, Marvin. *Legends of the Tennessee Vols*. Champaign, Ill.: Sports Publishing L.L.C., 2005.

-----. *Tales of the Tennessee Vols*. Champaign, Ill.: Sports Publishing L.L.C., 2001.